WINNING
LESSONS

WINNING LESSONS

From Corporate Life

O. P. Khetan

PARTRIDGE
A Penguin Random House Company

To order additional copies of this book, contact
Partridge India
000 800 10062 62
orders.india@partridgepublishing.com

www.partridgepublishing.com/india

CONTENTS

FOREWORD

When O. P. Khetan, my former colleague in the Rourkela Steel Plant, requested me to write the foreword for his book, "Winning Lessons from Corporate Life", I was only too happy as it is a rare privilege.

The book contains nuggets of wisdom on different social and managerial skills. The author has gathered them from his varied experience in the Public Sector steel plants at Rourkela, Durgapur and Head Office of Hindustan Steel Ltd. at Ranchi as well as at ICI India, a leading multinational company with presence in India even when the British ruled over us.

In January 1973, when I joined as the Town Administrator of the Rourkela Steel Plant, on deputation from the Government of Odisha, O. P. Khetan was the Head of Personnel Department of the plant with about thirty-three thousand workforce. In my experience, he has been one of the most outstanding shop-floor negotiators with leaders of trade unions. His most important trait has been his totally "cool persona". He would always listen to the Union Leaders with utmost patience. Often, I got the impression that just by listening patiently to the Union Leaders – and not interrupting them even once – he would literally tire them out. The net outcome of shop-floor negotiations would be a package of benefits for workmen which would be just, fair and reasonable. In other words, O. P. Khetan never yielded to the pressure tactics of the militant Union Leaders. He also did his best not to support the managements' unreasonable expectations from the workmen.

The author has also mentioned in his book that a solution to the dispute between management and workmen must result in a "Win-Win" solution for both. He has rightly stated that the trust of the workmen in the bona fides of the management is the basic requirement of a motivated workforce, and admittedly, a motivated workforce is essential for higher production and greater productivity.

In his book, the author has given a lot of importance to a host of human traits known collectively as Emotional Quotient or E.Q. He has mentioned that the team of Daniel Goleman and David C. McClelland from the Harvard University, has research data to prove that for a successful manager, Emotional Quotient or E.Q. is more important than Intelligence Quotient or I.Q.

Let me conclude. The book "Winning Lessons from Corporate Life" – which I have read in manuscript form many times over because of its anecdotal style and elegant prose – is a "must – read" for student of management and also professional manager.

P.C. Hota IAS (Retired)
Former Secretary to Government of India,
Department of Personnel & Training and
Former Chairman,
Union Public Service Commission.

New Delhi
1st January 2015

PREFACE

Why and how this book was conceived and written

The main purpose of this book is to help you in your social and work life and to solve your problems through tried and tested methods. The suggestions and ideas in the book are not based on theories but on my real life experiences over five decades. This includes over three decades as a management practitioner in two large corporations - Steel Authority of India (SAIL) and ICI India, a British multinational and experience of two decades of conducting soft skills training programmes.

After retirement in the year 1991 I have been conducting soft skills training programmes for managers, senior executives and supervisors at the leading hotels in New Delhi. In addition I have also conducted similar in-house training programmes for over 100 leading companies. By now more than 10,000 persons with varied educational background and experience have attended these programmes. Further, for more than two decades I had also been a Visiting Professor at the 'FORE School of Management' located at New Delhi's Qutab Institutional area and taught 'Human Resource Management' to the students of the MBA programme.

In all these programmes I found that the question & answer part of the session was the most interesting and sought after. Participants were hungry to get solutions to their problems which they faced in their day to day work life. The solutions had to be tried and tested. I found that these solutions and suggestions were more convincing and acceptable if these were based on a real life experience rather than on any theory of management. Most of my soft skills seminars were repeated many times over with an excellent feedback from the participants.

Gradually an idea started taking shape in my mind. Why don't I try to recollect all such experiences, classify them and present them in the form of a book? This book is the end result of this thinking. All examples given in the book are real life examples. In many cases the persons referred to are still working. Real names and places have been mentioned in most cases. But in some cases I have changed or omitted them to preserve anonymity.

During my professional career I had the good fortune of coming in contact with India's who's who, including cabinet ministers, ICS and IAS bureaucrats, corporate leaders, Secretaries to the Government, Army Generals as well as foreign nationals of more than a dozen countries. That gave me the variety and made the experiences and lessons all the more interesting and useful. Since the book narrates experiences of over five decades it is likely that the dialogues and details may not be very accurate. But these do not affect the basic theme and the lessons drawn. The examples and suggestions in the book are equally applicable to business as well as social life.

If by the time you have finished reading a few chapters of this book, you don't have the urge to go through the rest or you don't think the time was usefully spent, then I shall consider this book to be a failure.

O.P. Khetan

ACKNOWLEDGEMENTS

This is not a book. It is my dream come true, made possible by many. I thank all of them from the bottom of my heart.

My family members have contributed a great deal. My wife Hem Prabha encouraged me and supported me to fulfil my dream. My daughter Alka who stays in Dubai helped in selecting the publisher and my grandson Yuvraj helped me in editing. My grandson Jawahar who is studying at Purdue University U.S.A. prepared the basic design for the front and back covers. The maximum contribution in making this book a reality has been made by my son Alok who has devoted long hours out of his busy life and painstakingly edited the whole script improving and correcting my poor language and grammar. His efforts are all the more praiseworthy as he has a full time job with a British Multinational, Johnson Matthey.

I would particularly like to mention Mr. P. C. Hota IAS (retd.) who has been my friend philosopher and guide ever since I came in his contact in 1973 after he joined as Town Administrator of Rourkela Steel Plant on deputation from the Odisha Government. He has meticulously gone through the manuscript, edited and polished it. He has also written a superb foreword paying handsome tribute to me. I shall ever remain grateful to him.

I can't forget thanking all those real life actors quoted in this book. Without them playing their part in the various examples and incidents quoted, this book could not have been conceived and written.

I am happy that one of the best international publishers, PARTRIDGE, a Penguin Random House Company has agreed to publish this book. They have done a highly professional job of converting my script into a first rate self-improvement book. Thank you Team PARTRIDGE.

And lastly the tremendous help I received from Microsoft in the form of MS Office Word in checking the grammar and spellings when I was composing the script. Thank you Bill Gates.

O.P. Khetan

CHAPTER 1

Leading from the front

*"Management is doing things right;
leadership is doing the right things".*
Peter Drucker

Every year 15th August used to be a special day for the workers of the factory. It was the factory of ICI India producing industrial explosives. ICI India was a subsidiary of a British Multinational located in the interiors of Jharkhand at Gomia. Flag hoisting, speeches and distribution of sweets were all part of the festivities. But what had become a special event was the inter-departmental tug of war. Rehearsals of the festivities used to start months before. It was a prestige issue among the different departments of the factory. In the past the administration department, with a large contingent of security staff, used to be the winner.

After a few months of my joining, a young manager named Daljit Singh joined as Assistant Manager Blasting Dept. (I understand he is presently working as President of Fortis Healthcare Limited.) He was a top class sportsman. Earlier in another of our factory at Rishra (West Bengal) where I was also posted he used to win all the sports prizes during the annual sports event, so much so that we had to restrict him to five events and he would get gold medals in all those events.

Daljit must have heard from the workers about the tug of war among departments of the factory. He may have found this an opportunity to raise his own workers' morale. Most of the workers felt that it was difficult to beat the hefty security people forming the administration team. But Daljit had a vision. He must have felt that this was a God sent opportunity to try all that he had learnt about leadership at IIT Delhi and management training at ICI.

He called a meeting of the workers and told them that this year their department must win the tug of war. He selected a group of about 20 workers with the best physique and a desire to win. He made two teams from among them and started the practice sessions after the shift closing time. I got to know of this later. I do not know how long the practice and rehearsals lasted, but on the D-day, Daljit was at the head of the blasting team with the rope in his hand. Never before in the history of the tug of war at Gomia had even a supervisor taken part, much less a manger. It used to be mainly a workers' event.

Before the event started Daljit took the team aside and must have given them a pep talk. I overheard some of them saying "Aaj hamare sahib hamare sath hain aaj hame koi nahi hara sakta" ("Today our manager is with us so no one can defeat us") they came back and put their hands on the rope. The administration department was confident that as in the past they were going to win. However once the whistle blew the administration department pulled the rope for some distance, may be the momentum or confidence of the past, but then Daljit shouted "Bahaduro Aaj ijjat ka sawal hai, Khincho" ("Brave hearts, today it is a matter of prestige, pull"). For a moment the rope halted and then slowly but surely it started creeping towards the blasting department and continued. Finally the Blasting department had won and Daljit became an instant hero. He at once grew from a manager to a leader.

The other episode of leading from the front that I remember happened when I was working at the Durgapur Steel Plant of SAIL located in West Bengal. General Wadhera was the Managing Director and A K Pal IPS of the West Bengal cadre of the rank of DIG was on deputation as the Chief Security Officer of the steel plant. The CITU Union was the majority Trade Union. Relations of the management with CITU Union were extremely confrontationist and unusually tense.

On the fateful day, the CITU Union wanted to meet General Wadhera but he was very upset with them due to their agitational approach. He asked Pal the Chief Security Officer to ensure that they did not enter his office.

A contingent of U.P. Provincial Armed Constabulary was permanently posted at Durgapur and was at the command of Pal. When the CITU Union wanted to force their entry to the MD's Office Pal had no option but to order firing inside the admin building. Luckily no was killed or even hurt. But a hush fell on the waiting workers and the news spread like wildfire in the plant. About 10,000 shift workers surrounded the administration building and started burning the cars parked at the ground level in the administration building. They also started shouted slogans threatening the management with dire

The demand of the CITU Union was that A K Pal who had ordered the firing should be arrested and a case should be filed against him. But General Wadhera's stand was that since Pal had opened fire only to obey his orders he takes full responsibility for the action of A K Pal. Ultimately it was decided to have a meeting with the Senior West Bengal Govt. Officials at Assansol to sort out the matter. This is all what we heard later. I do not know how much of this was true. But this one episode raised Gen. Wadhera's image many steps up among the managers and right thinking employees of Durgapur Steel Plant.

The next instance of leading from the front came my way when I was working at Rourkela Steel Plant of SAIL located in Orissa. One night there was a heavy down pour of rain causing the roof collapse of the Steel Melting Shop which was the nerve centre of the plant. It caused serious damage to the plant resulting in its closure. It happened due to the callousness of the concerned mangers. Heavy iron and coal dust used to collect on the roof for which there was a procedure of periodical cleaning. It transpired that the cleaning was neglected for long periods and that night the roof could not bear the heavy load of iron dust soaked with water for long and gave in. The Steel Ministry took a serious view of this lapse and many heads rolled including that of the General Manager.

The Deputy Chief Engineer in charge of civil construction B L Khatri was given the task of rebuilding the roof. On the very first day he ordered a camp cot near the site and remained in the plant day and night 24 hours a day and never went home for the next couple of months till the job was over. As a result the tight deadline was not only met but the job was done before it. In recognition Khatri was elevated and his team duly rewarded. By leading from the front Khatri set an example which became a landmark for others to emulate.

The lesson is: If you want to be a successful leader of your team you must lead from the front and set an example for others.

CHAPTER 2

The Importance of Networking

"Pulling a good network together takes effort, sincerity and time."
Alan Collins,
author of "Unwritten HR Rules"

During the early part of my career I was posted at the head office of Hindustan Steel (earlier incarnation of SAIL) at Ranchi. My responsibilities included organisation structure, incentive schemes, job evaluation system, wage structure and allied matters. One day I was in my office engrossed in some important matter. Suddenly when I lifted my head I saw the CEO of Bhilai Steel Plant Mr. Purtej Singh standing in front of me. I was startled to see him in my office as he was many levels senior to me and easily 25 years older. I suddenly got up and told him "Sir you could have called me to your visiting office upstairs".

He waved his hand, sat down in an ordinary chair in front of me and also asked me to sit down and relax.

The conversation started. He asked me whether I went to the temples. I could not understand the relevance or the context of the question, but to be on the safe side told him that yes I used to visit along with my father in the past. Then he asked me what I did there. I said we used to pay homage to the main deity. He asked "after that?" I thought for a while and then as a rescue act replied that after that we used to go round the temple and pay homage to other deities. He stopped me then and there and said "Khetan I am doing the same thing. I have met the chairman (M S Rao ICS) and your Chief upstairs and I am going round and meeting the smaller deities like you in the Head Office so that my proposals are not held up." After almost 50 years of the incident I still admire the practical approach of Mr. Purtej Singh. No wonder the proposals of Bhilai Steel Plant were always processed speedily by the head office.

I got the opportunity to use the networking in my next assignment at Rourkela Steel Plant of SAIL where I worked as Head of HR. In those days due to the sophisticated plant technology we used to employ a large number of German Technicians and also used to send many of our engineers for training to Germany. Once we wanted to send about half a dozen engineers to Germany for a new plant that was coming up. The clearance from Steel Ministry was getting delayed. Mr. R. P. Sinha the CEO of Rourkela steel plant was a worried man. He called me to his office and asked me whether I could do something to hasten up the process. I suddenly remembered that the Joint Secretary concerned in the Steel Ministry used to visit Rourkela and was fond of playing bridge, and being a keen bridge player myself, whenever he visited Rourkela I would organise a bridge session in the evening at the Rourkela Club.

I told Mr. Sinha that I would visit Delhi the next day and try my luck. Same evening I caught the train to Kolkata and next morning a flight to Delhi. By 11.00 o'clock I was in the office of the Joint Secretary concerned. He was surprised to see me as I had no appointment with him but asked me the purpose of my dash to Delhi. In fact I still remember his words. He asked me "Khetan what has happened? Is everything OK at Rourkela?" I replied that everything was fine and I had come to seek a little help - clearance of our proposal for foreign training. Jokingly I told him that I would leave his office only after he gave me a formal letter of approval. He smiled and called his Deputy Secretary and Section Officer. They told him that the proposal was OK as far as the Steel Ministry was concerned but was held up by the Finance Ministry. He rang up someone in the Finance Ministry and to cut a long story short by the afternoon with the approval letter in my hand I flew back to Kolkata and the next morning handed over the letter to Mr. Sinha.

The importance of networking was reconfirmed when I left SAIL and joined ICI India. It also meant my moving from Rourkela (Orissa) to Kolkata. My son Alok had to be admitted in a good school. I was keen on La Martiniere, the leading school in Kolkata. I visited the school and met Dr. Raj the Principal but he flatly refused saying there was no vacancy. In my subsequent visits, the peon knowing the purpose would not even allow me to meet the Principal. After many such attempts failed, I approached our Managing Director Mr. Raghvan. He called the Administration Manager Stan Naidu and asked him to help. Stan fixed up an appointment for the next day. Next day, Stan and I along with my son went to La Martiniere and as soon we approached the Principal's Office the same peon saluted Stan and we went in and met Dr. Raj. His behaviour was different. He said yes he could admit my son but the boy would have to pass the test mandatory for all aspirants for admission to the school to judge his suitability. I readily agreed, my son passed the test was admitted. So easy now and so difficult earlier, all due to the magic of networking. Later I came to know that Stan Naidu was ICI's nominee on the La Martiniere's Management Committee. In fact after a year I replaced Naidu on the committee.

The next episode of using networking came my way after I was transferred from Kolkata to one of the factories in Jharkhand (earlier Bihar) at Gomia. During my working with HSL/SAIL at Ranchi my boss was Mr. Ramanand Sinha a senior IAS Officer of the Bihar cadre on deputation to Hindustan Steel (SAIL) who on reversion to Bihar Government became Additional Chief Secretary. I remembered my old boss Mr. Sinha who had retired by then and settled at Patna. During my next visit to Patna I met him at his house. He was very happy to see me. I told him that I was now working in Bihar and wanted his blessings. He smiled and asked me what I wanted. I requested him to introduce me to the senior IAS Officers concerned such as the Collector and Commissioner concerned and also the Labour Secretary and Labour Commissioner and Chief Secretary. Next day he took me to the Secretariat at Patna and introduced me to the concerned Officers telling them "Khetan is my boy". Thereafter I had no problem with the Bihar bureaucracy as long as I was at Gomia.

The last instance of networking that I remember took place when I had gone to Shimla for some personal work. I stayed there for a day and was ready to check out from the hotel. Suddenly I remembered that my old boss Mr. A N Banerji IAS(retd.) was the Governor of Himachal Pradesh. In fact he was my boss thrice. First time when I was working as a Junior Engineer at Durgapur Steel Plant he was the Deputy General Manager, second time he was the General Manager Rourkela Steel Plant and third time when I was at the Head Office of HSL at Ranchi he was the Deputy Chairman. So I decide to try my luck. From the hotel I rang the Raj Bhawan telephone number and asked for the ADC to the Governor. It was around 11.00 a.m. The ADC came on line. I informed him who I was and requested for a courtesy call on the Governor for a few minutes. I also told him that my wife and I were on our way back to Delhi and had checked out from the hotel. The ADC asked me to hold the line and came back in a minute saying that the Governor was willing to see me just now. It was too good to expect. Anyway the ADC asked for my car number and I along with my wife reached the Governor's Office without any problem. We met the ADC who asked us to wait and offered us tea/coffee. And also said that the Governor was very busy and had given only ten minutes. We were soon ushered into the Governor's chamber. He was very courteous and started talking about the old days of Durgapur, Rourkela and Ranchi. We kept on listening. Time flew. Half an hour went by. His ADC came in and perhaps reminded him about the next appointment. We got up, but before we left the Governor asked me, and I still remember his words "Khetan what can I do for you?" I was overwhelmed and replied "Sir thank you very much for giving us so much of your precious time. This is all what we wanted. We are just leaving Shimla for Delhi. Thank you very much". Saying so we left his chamber. But I am certain that if we needed any help at Himachal Pradesh with the bureaucracy Mr. Banerji would have surely tried to help us.

All the above real life incidents confirm the lesson: If we want to succeed in work life as well as social life networking can be of great help.

CHAPTER 3

Customer is King

"A customer is the most important visitor on our premises. He is not dependent on us. We are dependent on him...."
Mahatma Gandhi

In those days I used to conduct most of my HRD Centre's management training programmes at Delhi's Maurya Sheraton Hotel. In one of the programmes for top managers on 'Leadership & Teambuilding' I invited Mr. Nakul Anand the Vice President of ITC in charge of the Maurya Sheraton Hotel for a guest lecture. He readily agreed and delivered an excellent talk. At the end we had a question answer session. One of the participants asked:

"Mr. Anand what are you looking for to achieve in this hotel, I mean what is your goal"

Nakul Anand paused for a while and then said

"This is a good question. Well I am looking for simple 'Wows' from my clients".

"Sir what does that mean". Another participant quipped.

"I will explain it" said Nakul Anand.

"When the client disembarks from his limousine in my porch and looks around I want to hear him exclaim 'Wow', when he enters the hotel lobby and looks around I want to hear from him 'Wow', and when he goes up the elevator and enters his suite, I again want to hear 'Wow', This is my goal and this is what I constantly try to achieve in this hotel".

These words keep ringing in my ear even after 20 years. In these three 'Wows' Nakul Anand summed up the whole theory of customer satisfaction, customer delight and customer surprise.

To be true to this aim whenever I rang the Maurya Sheraton Hotel reception or the banquet sales the telephone was always lifted on the first ring, never the second. I must have rung them over 200 times during those seven years and not even once do I remember waiting for the second ring. Recently I read in the newspapers that President Obama of USA, after two nights stay complemented the hotel staff "Awesome hospitality ITC Maurya".

The same lesson "Customer is King" I learned during my days in ICI. We had started a new plant at Ennore near Chennai to manufacture the herbicide 'GRAMOXONE'. (This brand is now with Syngenta Corporation.) The sales team was recruited and they were to be given focused training to sell GRAMOXONE to farmers. We had asked Makhija, one of the famous trainers from Mumbai to conduct the training programme for our sales team. The programme was conducted at Taj Coromandal Hotel, Chennai and as Head of HR I went to oversee from the Kolkata Head Office.

Makhija organised a role play. He selected two participants at random to act as salesmen. One was to behave as he would do normally. The other participant was trained and briefed by Makhija in a separate room for around 15 minutes. A third participant was also briefed by Makhija separately to act as a wealthy farmer near Bangalore interested in horse racing and was in a hurry to leave for the race course that evening. The stage was set.

The first Salesman approaches the farmer.

"Sir I am from ICI. We make excellent herbicide GRAMOXONE, very good for your crops".

"What ICI and what GRAMOXONE, I am in a hurry to leave for the race course. Don't waste my time".

"Sir please five minutes. I will explain the benefits" tried the salesman.

"No no I have no time now, come some other time".

"Sir please, I have come all the way from Bangalore for you".

"So what? Did I tell you to come and see me? No more talk".

Makhija clapped and the role play was over.

The next salesman walks in. He has been briefed by Makhija to study the back ground of the farmer, his interests and his routine that day. Remember that the farmer was to behave as naturally as the real farmer would do in similar situation. The next salesman starts exactly the same way.

"Sir I am from ICI. We make excellent herbicide GRAMOXONE, very good for your crops".

"What ICI and what GRAMOXONE I am in a hurry to leave for the race course. Don't waste my time".

"Race course! That's great I am also going there after meeting you and I have got some tips as I know some people".

"What tips? You are just boasting to please me".

"No sir, as you know, in the last race that particular jockey was the favourite but he lost because of ......This time the most favourite jockey is such and such which is being kept secret".

"Are you sure?"

"Sir I am not 100% sure but the inside news is ...."

"OK OK how are you going to Bangalore".

"Sir I will hire a taxi although it is a big drain on me but it is my passion".

"Why don't you come with me in my car? We can also discuss your so called tips and your herbicide".

This time Makhija kept quiet but all the participants clapped instantaneously.

The role play was a hit. Everyone agreed that for a successful sales call, one must collect all relevant details of the customer beforehand, such as his background, his interests, and his routine that day.

My next experience took place in Kolkata. I had gone to the New Market to buy some toiletries. It was a small shop and the salesman looked like a middle aged modern owner. I asked in English "Can you show me some good shaving creams?" "Sure sir" he replied and spread about half a dozen on the counter. While I was looking at the spread, I overheard a feminine voice in chaste Bengali and saw a lady speaking "Lakmer bottereesh namber lipstick aache ki?" (Do you have Lakme no. 32 lipstick". I also heard the reply in chaste Bengali. "Hain, aekhuni dekhachee aapnake" (Yes, I will show you just now). A few minutes later I saw an old person in dhoti and kurta entering the shop. He asked "Bhaya ek lux sabun ke tikki dena" (brother give a cake of lux soap). The salesman replied "Babuji yeh lijiye". (Sir here it is). Whatever language the customer spoke the salesman replied in the same language!

These three real life episodes taught me the following lessons:

1. **Customer is King.**
2. **Speak the language of the customer.**
3. **Talk in terms of his interests rather than your own.**

CHAPTER 4

Where there is a will there is a way

"You will never do anything in
this world without courage"
Aristotle

When I was working as Head of Personnel at Rourkela Steel Plant of SAIL my colleague N K Singh was the Head of Personnel at Bhilai Steel Plant. There, at one time, late coming had become a practice as no action had been taken for long. Earlier various managements had tried to stop this practice but without any success. After N K Singh took over as Head of Personnel he was asked by the top management to enforce punctuality in a time bound manner. He discussed the matter with all concerned including the Union leaders. Most of them said it was difficult to break the old habit of late coming. The old timers said it had been tried earlier but it had not succeeded. Some even said that it had become a custom and practice.

After hearing all the concerned people Singh worked out an action plan in consultation with his senior HR colleagues and positive minded line managers. A well drafted circular went out in the first week of December mentioning about the provisions of the Standing Orders, the undesirable practice of late coming and its impact on production and productivity. The circular also stated management's resolve to enforce punctuality and the plan to take disciplinary action on defaulters from 1st January. This was followed by two more circulars in succeeding weeks stating the resolve more and more forcefully. The last circular was issued during the last week of December. All circulars were in both the languages - English and Hindi and were prominently displayed on all the notice boards of the plant.

Then on 1st January in the three shifts 6.00 a.m., 2.00 p.m. and 10.00 p.m. and general shift at 8.00 a.m. a large number of managers stood at the gate with a pad and pen in their hands. They started noting down the names of late comers. On the first day itself the number of late comers had reduced to almost half as a result of the circulars. After seeing that the names were being noted down the number further came down on the second day. This practice continued for three days. On the fourth day the number had dwindled to a very few and to these workers warning letters were issued. Still there were a few defaulters against whom disciplinary action was initiated. In a nutshell, punctuality was restored without any industrial relations problems.

The second instance of 'where there is a will, there is a way' was in a completely different situation. When I was posted at Kanpur as General Manger (HR) at ICI's Panki factory I was staying at Swaroop Nagar, a posh locality of Kanpur. Once there was a dacoity in my house. The police did a good job and caught the dacoits but could not recover the booty. The house was insured and I made a claim of Rs. 40,000 with the insurance company. I had completed all the requirements of the claim but the insurance company was not releasing the payment. The agent felt that if I paid the speed money it might help. I was in no mood to do so. In the mean time I had been transferred to Delhi.

Even after the transfer I used to visit Kanpur for official work. During one of those visits I went to the office of the insurance company at Meston Road and went straight to the Branch Manager (BM) Mr. Khan. He looked to be a well-built Pathan. I told him who I was and what the problem was. He patiently heard me and asked me "Do you have about an hour or so". By then I was fed up of chasing. So I said "yes no problem". He called the dealing assistant and asked him to bring the case file. The assistant wasn't very happy but he brought the file anyway. The BM went through the case, saw all the papers and after satisfying himself asked the assistant to process the case for his approval. The assistant said "Sir this will require approval of Head office at Delhi". The

Branch Manager told him that he knew the rules better and asked him to complete the file and bring it for his approval. With great reluctance the clerk processed the case with all the relevant documents and notings and brought the file. The BM again went through the papers quickly, gave his written approval for payment and asked for preparation of the cheque. Again the clerk said "Sir the cheque writer has not come to the office yet". The BM asked his Secretary to give a ring to the cheque writer to reach the office quickly.

To cut the story short the Branch Manager handed over the cheque to me after about one and a half hours. I thanked him profusely. I am sure after meeting me the BM must have realized that this was a genuine case and decided to assert his authority.

The third incident that I recall also took place at the Kanpur Fertilizer plant of ICI India. A new CEO, Thampi had taken over. He was a stickler for punctuality. He would always be in his office by 8.00 a. m. when the factory siren was still ringing. This forced the late coming managers to fall in line. Some of them who were habitual late comers did not like it. After couple of days of Thampi's joining they told him that while all other managers had fallen in line, one senior manager 'Satish' (name changed) was always late. Hearing this Thampi said 'Is that so?' and decided his action plan.

Next day at 8.a.m. Thampi was in Satish's office, which was nearby, and sat down on Satish's chair. He informed his Secretary accordingly. Some of the senior managers were watching the fun quietly from behind closed doors. When Satish came as usual around 8.30 a.m. he found the big boss sitting in his chair. You can imagine the plight of Satish and the dialogue which would have taken place. What we heard on the grapevine was that Thampi told Satish that if he was ever late in the future his chair would be occupied forever. It hardly needs mentioning that Satish was never late as long as Thampi was the CEO.

The lesson I learned from these episodes is: Where there is a will there is a way.

CHAPTER 5

How to motivate people

*"Management is nothing more than
motivating other people."*
Lee Iacocca

Most of the management students and practitioners are
aware of various theories of motivation by Abraham
Maslow, Hertzberg, Macgregor, McClelland and others.
I had the good fortune of attending a training programme
by David McClelland of Harvard University when he
visited India. I was highly impressed by his theory of need
for achievement, need for affiliation and need for power.
Later when I used to visit the Management Training
Institute of SAIL at Ranchi I came across an excellent
questionnaire combining the theories of Maslow and
McClelland.

The questionnaire is simple but the results that I used
to get were startling. I must have used it in over 100

soft skills training programmes that I have conducted by now easily covering over 1,500 participants and in most cases it was possible to predict the dominant need which motivates the person. The needs are classified as follows:

1. Basic needs   Need for survival, security, pay and comfort at work
2. Affiliation needs   Need for acceptance and appreciation by others
3. Achievement needs   Need to do own job well and achieve good results
4. Power needs   Need to influence and control others

Managing and leading a team of people with different personalities is never easy. It helps to know what motivates them, and what tasks fit them well. If we can know their dominant need it is so much easier.

In one leadership and teambuilding programme that I conducted in Manali (Himachal Pradesh) I used this questionnaire. The scores were extremes in the case of two participants. In one case – I still remember his name was Navneet Kapoor and he was working with Bharti Telenet at Shimla, the basic needs was showing an unusually high score. I asked him "Kapoor, are your basic needs high?" He replied without any hesitation. "Yes sir". I continued "why". He said "Sir Money is everything in this world. I want to earn as much as I can". The scores were confirmed.

In the case of another participant, B. N. Patro working with the National Institute of Rural Development, Hyderabad, I was surprised to see the basic needs score was unusually low. I repeated the same question to him. "Patro, are your basic needs low?" He said "yes sir". Again I asked "why". His reply was extremely interesting but truthful. He said "Sir, I belong to Orissa. My father is a famous advocate at Cuttack. He makes loads of money. I am the only son. He keeps sending more money than I need. So all my basic needs are more than fulfilled. Again the scores were confirmed.

As I mentioned earlier, I must have administered this questionnaire to over 1500 participants by now and the scores have always predicted the dominant need correctly. Apart from the highly professional design of the questionnaire I found that it was impossible to fudge it.

What is the learning and what is the practical use of all this? Let us take a simple example from the shop floor. You have two workers, one whose achievement needs are dominant. Let us call him "Achiever". The other's affiliation needs are dominant. Let us call him "Affiliator". Suppose there is a breakdown in the plant and you need someone to stay beyond normal working hours to ensure quick resumption. You approach the "Achiever'. The reaction will be "yes boss don't worry, I will go home only after setting the thing right". If you approach the "Affiliator" the reaction could be "boss I have some social engagement this evening. Can you not ask someone else"? Even if he agrees reluctantly, his feeling will be "Kya musibat hai. Pata nahi yeh boss mujhi ko kyon pakadta hai". (Trouble again, I don't know why the boss asks only me to stay back)

Let us take the reverse case. Every year in most of the factories 17th Sept is celebrated as Vishwakarma Day. A photo or statue of lord Vishwakarma is installed at a prominent place and after Puja and Aarti, Prasad is distributed to all those present. This is mostly organised by the workers. So nearer the Puja day you ask the Achiever "can you organise Vishwakarma Puja this year?" The reaction is likely to be "Boss can you not give it to someone else, I am busy in commissioning this new machine" or something like that. On the other hand suppose you ask the Affiliator, the response is likely to be "Yes boss thank you, I will make sure that this year Puja arrangements are the best". Such responses are not imaginary. These are supported by my own experience.

Let me quote another instance. I was conducting a training programme called "Enhancing Managerial Effectiveness" for senior managers at the Management Training Institute of SAIL at Ranchi. In one of the programmes I found that an elderly manager had a very high score on Power Needs. He was close to retirement. I casually asked him "Are you planning to join politics after retirement?" I still remember his reply "Sir Aapko kaise pata laga? Hum ek party se MLA ki ticket ki koshish kar rahe hain." (Sir how did you find out? Yes, I am trying to get a ticket for MLA from one political party.) It startled me and my faith on this 'Motivation mirror exercise' as I call it, further strengthened.

One more real life example of motivation by dominant need fulfilment comes to my mind. In the early years of my career I was posted as a Junior Engineer in the machine shop of Durgapur Steel plant (DSP). Before that I was trained for a year in the machine shop of Gary Steel Plant of U S Steel Corporation at Gary (Indiana) near Chicago, USA. In DSP we had a large number of lathe machine operators. I still remember 'Datta' after more than 50 years. He would often tell me "Sir, give me the job that no one else can do". I would keep looking for the most complicated repair jobs for him. And the more the difficult job that was given to him, happier he would be, with the expression "Sir yeh job hamare layak hai". (This job is befitting my calibre) Plant and machinery of Durgapur Steel Plant was imported from U.K. But the replacement that Datta made was as good as or sometimes even better than the original. Datta's dominant need was achievement and he was hungry to get it fulfilled.

The last real life example that I remember is from the Honda Car Company located at Greater Noida near Delhi. I had conducted over 20 man management soft skill training programmes for their supervisors. In almost all the programmes I used the famous management game of tower building to show the importance of achievement motivation. This game is used internationally. In the simplified version that I used, three participants were asked to volunteer for three roles, a manager, a supervisor and a worker. The worker is required build a tower by placing one cubical block of around 1.5" over another, as many blocks as possible till the last one falls. He is blind folded and has to use his non-dominant hand i.e. if he is right handed, he has to use his left hand and if he is left handed then he has to use his right hand. The manager and the supervisor have to play their usual role in getting as high a tower as possible built by the worker. In doing so they can do anything they like except that they cannot touch the blocks and cannot touch the worker. Other than these two things they can do anything.

Since this game has been played internationally in several training programmes abroad, the records show that the maximum number of blocks kept one over the other are around 18 to 20. In one programme when I gave this information one of the highly motivated and competent supervisors got up and told me that he wanted to play the role of a supervisor and wanted to select his own worker from the group. I allowed him to do so. The role play and the game stated. He was in full command, kept his cool, guided the worker at each step, kept motivating and informing him about the progress and ultimately when the worker kept the 18th block on the tower and it did not fall, everybody clapped. I went to the person concerned and hugged him and congratulated him. I am sure that after he heard the international record of 18/20 blocks a strong urge went through him and motivated him highly to break or match the record.

The last example I would like to quote applies to most of us. My daughter Alka received a first class first in her B.Sc. Examination from Meerut University. The U.P. Government organised a function at Lucknow to award gold medals to all the recipients. The recipients included all those who got first class first in the Bachelor's as well as Master's degree examination of all the U.P. Universities numbering around 25 at that time. My daughter could not attend the function as she had got married in the meantime and moved to Pune. But as luck would have it I was staying at Kanpur during that time. I thought if my daughter can't attend the function at least my wife and I can attend and be part of the grand ceremony. So I contacted my co-brother Vinod Mittal a senior IAS Officer in the U.P. Government. He enquired from the concerned officer and informed me that yes we can attend the function like other parents and collect the gold medal at the end of the function.

On the scheduled day my wife and I went to Lucknow. The function was organised in a big hall. We took our seats in the parent's enclosure. The large number of chairs on the dais slowly started getting occupied. They were all Vice Chancellors of all the U. P. Universities numbering around 25. Lastly the Governor of Uttar Pradesh accompanied by the U.P. Education minister came and sat down. The function started with a brief speech by the Education Minister. After that a senior Officer of the Education Department starting calling the names of the recipients and their Universities one by one and the Governor started awarding the gold medals. I could see the pride and recognition and motivation writ large on the faces of the students as well as the parents. Think of it, 25 Vice Chancellors are watching you and you are getting the medal from the Governor. The recognition that the recipient students got was seen to be believed. What more can you look for as a motivator. Watching the whole function, even we got a great sense of pride and recognition and motivation. In fact my daughter got two gold medals one meant for the B.Sc. topper and the other for the girl student B.Sc. topper. Since she was the overall topper she was awarded both the medals. If was a great idea of the Uttar Pradesh Government to motivate the students and their parents.

The lessons from the above real life examples are:

1. **If you want to motivate people, try to ascertain their dominant need and then find a way to fulfil it.**
2. **Pride, challenge and recognition are good motivators.**

CHAPTER 6

The Magic of appreciation

"Appreciation is a wonderful thing.
It makes what is excellent in others belong
to us as well."
Voltaire

Dale Carnegie's book 'How to win friends and influence people' has been my guide all these years. Two of the 'Mantras' mentioned in the book are:

1. Give sincere appreciation as often as possible.
2. Avoid criticism as far as possible.

I have been using these guidelines in my soft skills training programmes. Once I was conducting a training programme for Supervisors of Escorts at Faridabad. It was a two day programme. In most programmes we conduct dummy role plays. But since it was a two day programme I decided to try a live role play. During the session on motivation I asked the participants "If your wife or mother has made a good meal this evening, give sincere appreciation and we will discuss the feedback tomorrow". All of them agreed.

Next day when the programme started I asked for the feedback. One participant said that his wife said "Yeh training ka asar lag raha hai". (This looks to be the effect of training) One other said "She was very happy and our strained relationship has mellowed down". Still a third said shyly that his wife was very happy and they really enjoyed being together after a long time. Another one said that his wife happily asked him "Aaj tabiyat to thik hai na. Pahle to aisa aapne kabhi nahi kaha." (Are you ok because earlier you never said anything like this) But one elderly participant Yadav gave a discordant note. He said "Sir aapne to hame marva dia". (Sir you got me into serious trouble) I was worried and asked him what happened. He said "Sir when I reached home I saw that my wife's brother was at home. So my wife had cooked a good meal. In the last 25 years of marriage I had never said anything good about food. But you forced me to appreciate. So I told my wife "Aj to bahut achha khana banaya hai". (Today you have cooked very good food). She took it as sarcasm and did not talk to me the whole night. There was laughter all around and after some discussion Yadav realised his mistake of not using common sense. After general discussion all agreed that sincere appreciation can be a good motivator.

The next experience relates to the opportunity I got to apply the mantra of sincere appreciation to get me out of a difficult situation. This happened when I was working as General Manager (HR) at one of the factories in Bihar. Our Trade Union had given a strike notice. The Labour Commissioner Madhav Sinha was on a field visit. We invited him as chief guest and organised a talk by him. The function was arranged in our Club Hall and over 200 managers and supervisors attended the programme. Sinha spoke well and was very happy to see the large audience. In the evening we discussed with him the strike notice and assured him that we were confident of handling it at our own level. However, in a few days the situation turned worse and I was given the job of dashing to Patna and getting help from the Labour Dept. Our local Liaison Manager Vijay Topa had alerted me that Sinha had already got the news and was very upset. I was at my wit's end.

Nevertheless I dashed to Patna and decided to try the mantra of sincere appreciation. As soon I entered Sinha's room and before he could speak anything I said in Hindi:

"Sir aapka lecture abhi tak gomiawale yad karte hai" (Sir People in Gomia still remember the excellent talk you gave the other day). He forgot all his anger and said (with happiness visible from his face) "Khetan Sahib aapne to bahut logo ko bula lia us din" (Mr. Khetan You called lot of people that day). Seeing his mood I continued "Sir we were constrained by our club hall capacity otherwise we would have invited many more". By that time his anger was gone and he said "OK tell me what the latest news is". After which we carried on our normal discussion and he promised all help by his officers.

My next opportunity to use Dale Carnegie's mantra also happened when I was working as General Manager (HR) with ICI at Gomia in Giridih District. We got involved in a court case and the next hearing was at the level of District Judge (DJ). My Administration Manager Hari Kishore had fixed a meeting with the DJ a day before. When we went to see him in his chamber I was surprised to see the grandeur. It was one of the most lavish chambers I had ever seen. So as soon as we entered and immediately after Kishore introduced me to the Judge, I said "Your lordship I have never seen such a beautiful chamber as yours in my whole life". The Judge was visibly happy and I still remember his reply. He said "Yes Mr. Khetan you are right, recently the Chief Justice of India was here and he also said the same thing". He kept on talking about his chamber and we kept on listening. This went on for about 20 minutes. We never raised the issue of our case. When we were about to get up, rather than our raising the issue, the Judge said "Don't worry about your case tomorrow". And on that note we shook hands and left his chamber.

During my soft skills training programmes many times the participants have asked me "Sir is this not flattery and sycophancy and can it not have an opposite effect?" The discussion then starts and rather than answering the question directly I go in a roundabout way. I ask them "Suppose you cut your finger by a vegetable knife.

Whose fault is it? Is it the Knife's? The answer obviously is that it is entirely the fault of the person using the knife. The same is true of appreciation. It is a powerful tool to motivate others but we have to use it properly otherwise it can hurt us. In using it remember the following three rules so that you don't hurt yourself.

Rule no. 1   Appreciation has to be sincere. No flattery or sycophancy.

Rule no. 2   Appreciation has to be timely. You can't say that the good work you did last month was excellent.

Rule no. 3   Appreciation has to be appropriate. There are many ways and levels of appreciation starting from a pat on the back to a letter of appreciation to financial rewards to promotion. You have to decide which one fits the occasion.

Also remember that while criticism must always be done privately, appreciation can either be done privately or publicly depending on whether it will motivate or de-motivate others.

The lesson from all the above examples is: Sincere appreciation is one of the best motivators.

CHAPTER 7

Anything worth doing is worth doing well

"The best prize that life has to offer is the chance to work hard at work worth doing"
Theodore Roosevelt

I was in a batch of 115 engineers trained in U S A by the Government of India under the Ford Foundation grant of $1.5 million. This training was for Public Sector Steel Plants at Rourkela and Durgapur. In USA we had an American Training Coordinator, Steve Blickenstaff. After completing one year's training we came back to India. I was posted at the Head Office in Ranchi. In the meantime Steve was appointed as the Chief Training Adviser of Hindustan Steel (SAIL) also at the Ranchi Head Office.

One day Steve rang me and told me that the Rotary Club of Ranchi had invited him to give a talk about the 'American way of life' and that he would like me to say a few words about my American training as a part of his presentation. I readily agreed. On the appointed day we went to the Ranchi Club where the Rotary Club meeting was fixed. I sat down in the audience. After the ceremonial formalities were over, Steve was introduced to the audience. It was now his turn to make a presentation. The year was 1960. No power point software was known by then and no LCD projectors were available. In fact even an overhead projector was not available in the Ranchi Club. So Steve did the next best thing. He made his visual presentation on chart papers.

On the day of presentation Steve pinned these charts on a black board. He started his talk impressively and supplemented it through the posters prepared on the chart papers. After he completed the first topic, instead of turning the sheet back he tore half the sheet through perforations. The top half of the chart paper remained the same but the bottom half was different. But the two together showed a different picture. Next time he tore off the right half of the top sheet vertically through perforations. He kept on doing this in various ways. The net impact was no less impressive than a power point presentation.

After the talk I asked him "Steve it must have taken you very long to make this presentation?"

He said "Yes it did"

"But why did you take so much trouble?"

His reply still rings in my ear "Khetan, I firmly believe that anything worth doing is worth doing well."

I said "Steve I am highly impressed but tell me how you got those perforations made in various directions?"

"Oh that my wife did with her sewing machine." He replied.

And I said "Steve hats off to you for your painstaking efforts."

My next experience happened during one of the in-house training programmes. Pepsi Foods (Frito-Lay) had asked me to conduct 'Leadership Development' programmes for their three factories at Patiala, Pune and Kolkata. It was a two-day programme at each location. For the Patiala programme I reached there on the previous night. Next morning I walked into the conference room which was in the same hotel. Their HR Manager Amitabh Sagar had arranged the venue perfectly. The layout of tables with name cards and proper audio visual aids were all kept ready. Participants started coming. They all reached before time which was not my usual experience. They came in their company jerseys. Their body language displayed their full enthusiasm for the programme. On a side table I saw many different prizes wrapped up properly.

So I asked Amitabh "What are these for?"

He said "Sir these are meant for the participants. Whenever anybody replies to your question correctly, or gives a good suggestion, or does well in a role play or any exercise, you can award the prize."

I asked him "But you have kept different types of prizes and so many?"

He said "These are all at your discretion. You can decide the prize based on the value of his contribution to the programme or his learning displayed and award the prizes liberally".

There must have been more than two dozen prizes, and every half an hour or so somebody or the other was receiving a prize with clapping all round. In my rating the programme at Patiala was one of the best in-house programmes that I have ever conducted in the past two decades. No wonder I have heard that the Patiala plant of Pepsico has been one of the best performing plants.

My next experience happened in a curious way. After retirement from ICI when I started the HRD Centre Mr. K L Puri former Chairman of NTPC was one of my star faculties. But once Mr. K L Puri himself organised a programme at Maurya Sheraton Hotel and asked me to oversee the arrangements to ensure that there were no problems. Mr Puri had issued invitations to a very large number of his contacts. It was not clear who would pay the fee and who were invitees. On the conference reception counter I saw a smart lady Swati Basu along with two of her assistants. The delegates were coming in droves as the programme starting time approached. Some were giving cheques, some did not know whether they were supposed to pay, some others were not in the list at all. Around 250 to 300 delegates must have come that day. Swati was handling the jamboree without any sign of tension or fatigue and with a high degree of efficiency.

When I started HRD Centre and started conducting open programmes at leading hotels in New Delhi in 1991, I was looking for a programme coordinator who could handle 40/50 participants. This involved welcoming them and asking for their business cards, getting the registration form signed, handing over folders, enquiring about the cheque in a subtle way, preparing the receipts for the cheques and escorting them to their seats in the conference room. Before the guests would start arriving she had to place the name cards in the proper order and ensure the proper seating layout. During the programme she would have to prepare a list of the questions raised by the participants, receive the guest faculty with all courtesy and look after their comfort. I found her doing all this and more with clinical efficiency. Once I asked her "Swati how you do all this?" Her reply was "Mr. Khetan, I enjoy doing it." This says it all.

The motto of all these people motioned above was, '**If anything is worth doing, it is worth doing well.'**

CHAPTER 8

Importance of listening and how to listen

"The most important thing in communication is hearing what isn't said".
Peter Drucker

During my tenure at Durgapur Steel Plant (DSP) of SAIL I had the rare opportunity of attending a meeting with Mr. Jyoti Basu, then the Dy. Chief Minister of West Bengal. A meeting was fixed with him at 12 noon in the Writers Building at Kolkata. The year was 1969. I was a member of the management team from Durgapur Steel Plant. Two other senior members were General Wadhera, Managing Director and S C Sarkar IAS Personnel Manager on deputation to SAIL. I was included in the team as an expert on incentive schemes. The Union side was represented by Ajit Mazumdar the local MLA and President of the CITU union and two or three workers of

DSP. The issue to be discussed was the incentive scheme of Wheel & Axle plant of DSP. We reached the Writers Building about fifteen minutes earlier, informed about our arrival to the Private Secretary (PS) to Mr. Basu and sat down in the waiting room. I started relaxing as I thought the meeting would be delayed.

Suddenly on the dot of 12.00 noon the PS walked in and asked us to follow him. We were ushered into the Dy. CM's room. Mr. Jyoti Basu was already in the chair. He motioned to Mazumdar to start. Mazumdar gave the full background of the problem, how in his opinion the present scheme was unworkable and should be modified to reduce the targets and how in spite of their taking up the issue with the management repeatedly the management was not listening and wanting to take action on the workers for no fault of theirs. The workers accompanying him supplemented in great detail the present incentive scheme and the changes required and various other wrong actions of the management.

The incentive scheme was not a simple thing to understand so quickly in one go. And I wasn't sure how much Mr. Jyoti Basu was absorbing. The other thought going through my mind was that a problem which should have been resolved, at best at the level of Personnel Manager has come to the level of Dy. Chief Minister. Anyway I had no alternative but to wait and watch and speak only when asked. The Union side kept on talking and blaming the management on various issues and this went on for about one and a half hours. Mr. Jyoti Basu kept on listening without uttering a word during all this period. When he found that Union side of the story is over he asked General Wadhera, MD to respond.

General Wadhera mainly confined himself to the importance of DSP in the national economy, the efforts of the management to improve production, productivity and discipline and the problems and indiscipline created by the CITU Union. He was supplemented by S C Sarkar IAS, the Personnel Manager. Sarkar mainly confined himself to the issue of indiscipline by CITU Union workers and the need to restore discipline in the plant. I was then asked to explain about the incentive scheme which I completed in about ten minutes. During all this period of about twenty-five minutes Mr. Basu kept on listening without speaking a word.

Around five minutes to 2 o'clock Mr. Basu motioned for us to stop. He told General Wadhera to look into the suggestions of the Union afresh and see what best could be done to resolve the conflict amicably. He then asked Mazumdar to go back to Durgapur and try to resolve the problem by discussions with the management and in the meantime ensure that there was no indiscipline. The meeting was over exactly at 2.00 p.m. Mr. Jyoti Basu had been only listening except for those last five minutes. But all those attending the meeting had full satisfaction that they had been heard and Mr. Basu had understood and absorbed all that was discussed.

Later we came to know from his PS that Mr. Basu came to our meeting straight from the cabinet meeting and he had to attend a party meeting starting at 2.00 p.m. Hats off to you Mr. Basu you taught me a lesson on importance of listening which I remember to this day.

The same lesson was repeated during one of my seminars. I was conducting a programme on 'How to manage contract labour, casuals etc. at Hotel Maurya Sheraton during October 1999. Forty participants attended the programme. A three member team from NIRMA including Karsanbhai Patel's son Rakesh also attended the programme. It was a three day programme. From 9.30 a.m. to 5.00 p.m. There were plenty of discussions and most of the time was spent on question and answer part of the sessions. However I found that while Rakesh listened to everything with rapt attention, he hardly spoke.

At the end of the programme I asked him "Rakesh, this is a rare opportunity for the participants to have you here. Nirma and Karsanbhai has been a model of success against tough competition. We are all interested to know what the secret of your success is." He thought for a while and then said "Hard work". These were the only two words he spoke in the entire programme of three days. Rakesh taught us without saying so, that for achieving success, listening is at least as important as speaking.

My next experience on importance of listening took place in an interesting manner. One HR professional Shekhar had been asking me for quite some time to use him as a faculty. So next time when an organisation wanted to conduct an in-house programme on listening skills I asked Shekhar to go ahead and have a meeting with Sharma, the HR Head of the organisation. But in the evening of that meeting I got a call from Sharma refusing to accept Shekhar as the faculty. The reason as quoted by Sharma "Sir he kept on talking during the entire meeting and did not allow me to speak. A person who doesn't know how to listen, can he be a good trainer on listening skills?"I agreed with him and replaced the faculty.

These experiences taught me the importance of listening but in most organisations the common complaint of the rank and file is "Is company mai koi suntan nahi hai. Bolne ka kya fayda" (Nobody listens in this company. What is the use of speaking) I heard it from the managers, workers and Union leaders during my service. And later I heard the same expression from the managers and supervisors who attended my soft skill programmes. Why is it so? The reasons are given by the behavioural science researchers. Research says that although we spend 45% of our waking lives listening, very few of us have ever been taught to listen. We only spend around 9% of our time writing, now even lesser with PCs and e-mails, yet writing is the most taught of the communication skills.

But how to be a good listener? The following suggestions may help.

- Build rapport by pacing the speaker.
- You have to be a whole body listener.
- You can't daydream with body here and mind elsewhere.
- Listen with your ears, your eyes and your heart.

CHAPTER 9

How to say 'NO' yet keep a good relationship

*"Learning to say no can earn you respect
from yourself as well those around you."*
Auliq Ice

One of the best answers to the above question was provided by Mr. Russi Billimoria, my boss as well as my friend, philosopher and guide. During his long career he occupied many important positions including Director (Personnel) and Chairman of SAIL and before that a long tenure in Tata Steel including Director (Personnel). In these positions it was natural that he would receive many requests for favours. I was a witness on some of these occasions. Whenever anyone asked for a favour and Mr. Billimoria was against it he would say with all seriousness "Bhaia hamari naukri chali jayagi" (brother I will lose my job) and invariably the matter would end then and there without spoiling the relationship.

After retirement when I set up the HRD Centre and started conducting management training programmes, once I invited Satish Pradhan to take a session in my programme. In those days Satish was working with ICI and later joined Tatas as HR Chief at Mumbai. Satish said "I would have loved to come but I am busy that day but no problem, I suggest you take Ram Kumar whom you will find better than me." In those days Ram Kumar was working with Satish at ICI. I understand these days Ram Kumar is the HR Chief at ICICI Bank. I invited Ram Kumar and he gave an excellent talk. My relationship with Satish remained as good as ever. In fact later after completing her management programme from Singapore Management University, when my granddaughter Akanksha was doing her internship with the Tatas at their Mumbai office Satish helped her a lot and even offered her a job if she wanted to join the Tatas.

Another instance that I remember happened when I was working as Personnel/HR Chief at Rourkela. An interview was being conducted by a panel headed by Mr. P C Hota IAS the Town Administrator on deputation to the Rourkela Steel Plant. I was under pressure from some political bigwig to select his candidate. I passed on the request to Mr. Hota. He said he would look into it. After the interview when I enquired about the particular candidate his reply was "Mr. Khetan I tried my best but he was so bad that if you were heading the panel you would have thrown him out of the room. I did not do so mainly because of you." I did not have courage to ask him anything further.

My next experience came about when I was working as General Manager (Personnel) at Kanpur. One Sunday the Director of Factories (DOF) dropped in at my residence at Swaroop Nagar. I knew him well but the visit was unannounced. As soon as he sat down his first sentence was "Aap meri bibi se mera talaq dilwa denge". (You will get me a divorce from my wife) I was worried and asked him what had happened. In a nutshell he explained that his wife's brother was unemployed and that she had given him an ultimatum to find him a good job. And since ICI was a good paymaster I must find a job for him. I was thinking of how to get out of the awkward situation. Suddenly I remembered my guru Billimoria and his rescue act. So I told the DOF that I had no powers of recruitment. All such powers were with the Chairman (which was true). And even if I tried to issue an appointment letter it would be cancelled the next day by the Head Office and in the process I would surely lose my job. I don't think he believed me and he was certainly not happy. But under the circumstance he had no alternative except to ask me to think it over. Saying so, he left very reluctantly.

During my various postings I found one Secretary did his job of protecting me from unwanted visitors very well. I was curious to know how he did it. So I asked him one day. He said his usual response was that "Mr. Khetan is not on the seat". This is a typical terminology used in public sector. However I wanted to explore more to test his competence. So I asked him "Suppose in spite of your reply the person walks into my office, opens the door, finds me there, talks to me and then walks to you from the other side and asks why you said no". His reply deserves full marks. He said "Sir I would tell him that when his telephone came the boss was not on the seat. The boss just walked in a minute ago". Good way to say no and escape. The visitor may not believe my Secretary's version but he has no way of knowing the truth.

Most of my postings were in places far away from the Capital of India and the capital of politicians. Towards the end of my career I was posted at the Kanpur fertilizer plant of ICI as Head of HR. One day in the office I received a call and the person on the other end asked authoritatively "Is Mr. Khetan on the line?" I replied "yes". "Please speak to the Minister of Fertilizer and Chemicals" the voice said. Before I could recover and compose myself another voice said. "Mr. Khetan you are having an interview today, select such and such a candidate". Many thoughts went through my mind with lightning speed. Was the call genuine? If it was genuine what happened if I kept quite or said no. Suddenly a spark came through my mind. I replied "Sir I am in a meeting, lots of people are in my room please ask your PS to give me your telephone number and I will ring you back immediately". The voice at the other end said "OK OK" and ended the call. I never got the telephone number nor heard from those voices. There were some more instances like this during my tenure at Kanpur. And till this day I have no means of knowing whether those calls were genuine or fake.

The art lies in saying 'no' and yet keep good relationships. If relationships are spoiled than the whole purpose is lost. Through my experience, I have compiled a few suggestions of saying 'no' which you may find useful.

- I am really not the most competent person to do the job.
- I am busy but why don't you ask such and such a person who will do a better job.
- I have some urgent family commitments right now.
- It is beyond my powers.
- I have not seen any such papers.

The lesson is this: If we have to say 'NO' we must find a way to do it in such a way that it doesn't spoil our relationship.

CHAPTER 10

How to motivate the team

"Coming together is a beginning.
Keeping together is progress.
Working together is success."
Henry Ford

"For this round of Tambola/Housie the prize for full house is $1,000", announced Mr. Narendra Chaudhary – the Chief of Mittal Steel at Galati (Romania). A hush fell over the crowd. The place was a cruise on the river Danube. The group consisted of over 50 Indian and Romanian managers of Mittal Steel and their families. The party was organised to bid farewell to Mr. Chaudhary and to welcome Mr. K A P Singh the new Chief. I was a witness to the drama in real life. The previous day, my wife and I had landed in Bucharest, the capital of Romania, a beautiful Eastern European country and driven to Galati - the steel town where my son-in-law

Sanjiv Goel was working as a General Manager with Mittal Steel.

Announcement of the $1,000 brought high excitement and motivated the whole group. Earlier, singing, dancing, eating and drinking, together by the Indian and Romanian managers and their families had gone on during the entire cruise ride from 1 p.m. till 11 p.m. I have never seen a more motivated group of managers. No wonder the Sidex steel plant at Galati – one of the largest steel plants in Eastern Europe - which was making a daily loss of one million dollars before the takeover by Mittal Steel made a profit of over $100 million in the first year after the takeover. Narendra Chaudhary, whom I knew from my Durgapur Steel Plant days, knew the art of team building and motivation to the hilt.

My next experience took place when I was working as the General Manager (Personnel and Admin.) at ICI's explosive factory in the interiors of Jharkhand at Gomia. Being an explosive factory it was located away from habitation. The nearby towns of Hazaribag, Giridih, Bokaro, Dhanbad and Ranchi were more than one and a half to two hours away. The factory had a large perimeter as the various units were located far away from each other to avoid impact in case of any unfortunate explosion. However, these conditions resulted in the plant having a large security force. Most of them were ex-servicemen. They had a tradition of celebrating BARAKHANA (literally - big meal) once a year. After my joining on the next BARAKHANA day the security department had organised a grand function and invited the senior managers with all the security staff and admin staff.

In the middle of the programme when the loud speakers were playing national songs, suddenly from behind, a young security guard lifted me and put me on his shoulder. I also saw that our CEO Thampi was similarly lifted by another guard and Vinod Bahri the Plant Chief by yet another guard. They started taking us around the ground like in Ramlila Hanuman lifts Ram and Lakshman. It was totally sudden and amusing, although our Security Officer Capt. Nautiyal had given me a hint that something like this might happen. They took us around the ground and then placed us on a stage set for their programme. After that they all started asking loudly "Thampi sahib panch hazar, Thampi sahib panch hazar". (Thampi Sir five thousand, Thampi Sir five thousand) Thampi did not understand Hindi so he asked me what it was all about. I asked Nautiyal and after hearing from him told Thampi that they want five thousand rupees for the celebration. After thinking for a minute Thampi said - tell them that I have granted ten thousand rupees. I looked at him to ascertain whether I had heard him correctly. He said "yes ten thousand". So I announced in Hindi "Aap log panch hazar mang rahe the Thampi sahib ne das hazar diye" (You people were asking for five thousand rupees, Thampi Sir has given ten thousand rupees.) You could have seen their jubilation. They shouted with as loud a voice as possible - "Thampi sahib ki jai, Thampi sahib ki jai". (Hail Mr. Thampi, Hail Mr. Thampi) This went on for quite some time.

Later, when Thampi was a little free from them we went aside and Thampi said "You must be wondering why I did this. Look we have received a strike notice from the Union. We need to keep our security force happy and committed. Rupees five or ten thousand is peanuts. So don't worry. Just find a way to give this benefit without any reaction from the other workers". In consultation with Nautiyal and our Administration Manager Kishore we gave them blankets (equivalent to their share of the amount) which they could use during night duty. The security team was highly motivated and remained so for quite some time.

Thampi had a knack of keeping his team highly motivated. In his next assignment as CEO of Kanpur Fertilizer plant whenever the plant broke the past performance record he would organise a grand party for the managers. The workers would be rewarded automatically through an incentive scheme.

I learned the next lesson about team motivation during one of the lecture meetings of the National Institute of Personnel Management at SCOPE Centre in New Delhi. We had invited Kapil Dev the cricket captain, after India had won the World Cup. He spoke very well. During the question answer session someone from the audience asked him "Mr Kapil Dev you have been a successful leader of the Indian cricket team. What is the secret of your success? He paused for a while and then replied in a mix of Hindi and Haryanvi "Oji secret kuch nahi hai. Jo hum jit kar aye to bando ko age kar dia ki jit inki vajeh se hui or agar har kar aye to mai age agaya aur bola ki har meri vajah se hui." (Look there is no secret. If we won then I would keep the team mates in the front and say that the victory was due to them and if we lost then I would come forward and accept full responsibility for the defeat.) There could not have been a better answer. Mr. Kapil Dev you knew the secret of team building and motivation to the hilt. No wonder it was under your leadership that India won the World Cup against heavy odds.

In a complete contrast I recently read in Sachin Tendulkar's book 'Playing it My Way' that Greg Chappell, the Australian Coach from 2005 to 2007 had a habit of doing the reverse. Tendulkar writes "I also remember that every time India won Greg could be seen leading the team to the hotel or into the team bus but every time India lost he would thrust the players in front". No wonder during his time India's 2007 World Cup campaign ended in a fiasco with the team winning only one of the three group matches against lowly Bermuda and losing to Bangladesh and Sri Lanka.

The lesson is: If you want to motivate your team give them due recognition, appreciation and reward.

CHAPTER 11

How to make the other person feel important

"You can make more friends in two months by becoming interested in other people than you can in two years by trying to get other people interested in you."
Dale Carnegie

A real life incident which I am going to narrate was told to me by one of my very good friends, V D Sharma, who was working as General Manager DCM Chemical Works at New Delhi. One day there was fire in the factory. Since the plant was in the capital of India, the news spread like wild fire through the TV channels. Sharma was at the factory. His wife was at home watching TV. Some news channels started reporting that the General Manager Sharma may be arrested due to his negligence. Mrs. Sharma was worried. As soon as she saw the news on

TV screen, she rang up her husband. When Sharma got the call, Lalaji, the owner (I don't remember his name but he was from the famous Shriram family) was sitting with Sharma. As soon as Sharma started talking to his wife, Lalaji understood who was at the other end. He asked Sharma to hand over the phone to him. Lalaji told Mrs. Sharma "Mrs. Sharma I am so and so and am sitting with your husband in his room. Don't worry. He is not at fault. Even then if the police come to arrest him they will have to arrest me first". The police never came. But Sharma told me that after that communication from Lalaji to his wife he was virtually sold out to him and could never think of leaving him or the organisation for any other organisation.

I had the next experience about the value of giving importance when I was working with ICI India. (Now Akzo Nobel) For the first three years, I was posted at Kolkata and then transferred to one of the factories in Jharkhand. Dr. Subrato Ganguli was the Director (personnel) and was my functional boss. Once he organised a party at his house in Kolkata on the occasion of Group Industrial Relations Conference. In accordance with the practice in the company, I received the invitation as Mr. & Mrs. O. P. Khetan. The party was scheduled for the following week, but I happened to be in Kolkata a few days earlier for another meeting. I met Dr. Ganguli and asked him "your invitation is addressed to my wife also. Do you want me to bring her along?" I still remember his reply. "Yes why not, the company plane is making a flight that day, bring her along." ICI had an 8 seater islander plane which used to do sorties between Gomia and Kolkata. On the party day my wife and I took the plane to Kolkata and returned the next morning. This one incident boosted my ego and my wife was on cloud nine.

Another experience that I remember took place when on the nomination by the Government of India I went to the U.K. for an advanced programme on Personnel Management and Industrial Relations. The programme included a study tour of British Steel Corporation at their Head Office at Grosvenor Place, London as well as their plants at Sheffield and Teesside. Later the corporation was merged with Corus which was acquired by Tata Steel in 2006. In those days I was working as Head of Personnel/HR at Rourkela Steel Plant of SAIL. When I went to the Head office of the British Steel Corporation, the receptionist was sitting in a big hall. I showed her my papers. She rang up someone and asked me to wait. Within a few minutes an officer from inside walked in, greeted me by name and requested me to follow him. I thought he may be either the Secretary or the assistant of the big boss. He took me to a real big and grand room and asked me to take a seat and he himself sat down on the boss's chair. Only then did I realise that he was the boss and he had escorted me from the receptionist to his room. After completing the day's discussion he escorted me back to the car, opened the car door for me and then said goodbye. The importance I received at the British Steel Corporation will remain in my memory for ever. In fact after that visit I started following a similar protocol for all important guests.

My next experience was when I was working as Head of Personnel and administration at one of the factories of ICI. Mr. P. M. Thampi was the Plant Head. Dr. S S Baijal was the MD and Mr. A L Mudaliar was the Chairman. A meeting of the management committee was held at Gomia on 14th August 1980 attended by the Chairman and MD along with Mr. Thampi and other Plant Heads. Next day the Chairman and the MD were to leave for Kolkata by the company plane but due to the bad weather they could not leave. The day was 15th August and traditionally the Plant Chief used to do the flag hoisting. But since the MD and the Chairman happened to be in town, I, as in charge of the arrangements requested, first the Chairman and then the MD to hoist the flag. But both declined politely stating that as in the past it was only appropriate that the Plant Chief hoists the flag. What they really said, without saying so, in so many words was that the Plant Chief must be given his due importance.

One other incident, though a minor one, always remains in my mind. Once I was travelling to Kolkata in the company plane with my boss Mr. Shiven Verma and his wife. I was booked to stay in the company guesthouse. In the plane Shiven asked me where I would be staying. When I mentioned the guesthouse he said - no you are going to stay with me at my house. I had no choice. When we got down from the plane there was one car which was to take Mr. & Mrs. Verma to their house and then drop me at the guest house. When we approached the car I was waiting for Shiven and his wife to get in and sit in the back seat so that I may sit in the front. But Shiven sat down in the front seat and asked me to sit in the back with his wife. I was rather uncomfortable but Shiven would not listen and ultimately I had to sit in the back seat. His gesture, however, boosted my ego.

Why do I remember all these experiences? Because these made others and me feel important, boosted our ego and motivated us.

The lesson is simple: If you want people to like you and to have good relationship with you, give them due importance and do it sincerely.

CHAPTER 12

Effective decision making

"Once we decide we have to do something,
we can go miles ahead"
Narendra Modi

There are numerous decision making styles and practices. Three important requirements of an effective decision are quality, process and speed. I am quoting below my real life experience in the hope that these may help you in your own decision making.

My first major learning about decision making took place when I was working as a Junior Officer at the Head Office of Hindustan Steel Ltd. (HSL/SAIL) at Ranchi. The occasion was the farewell of Mr. M. S. Rao, I.C.S., Chairman of HSL. Mr. Prakash Tandon, Chairman of Hindustan Lever, who was also a Director of HSL was presiding over the function. What struck me at that young age was the appreciation bestowed by Mr. Tandon on the decision making style of Mr. Rao. Mr. Tandon said that the decision making style of Mr. Rao during the HSL Board meetings was such that they always felt as if they were taking the decision although they knew that the decisions were of Mr. Rao.

A few months earlier I had the good fortune of witnessing the style of Mr. Rao first hand. One morning I got a call from his Private Secretary (PS) to attend a meeting in the Chairman's office at 11 a.m. It was unusual for a Junior Officer like me to be called for a meeting with the Chairman. My enquiries from the PS about the purpose did not elicit much information. Anyway, when I entered his office I saw the Director (Finance), Director (Tech) and my own boss already there. As soon as I sat down, Mr. Rao mentioned the issue and asked for my opinion. I thought for a few seconds and then gave my opinion. After hearing my views he started asking others, one by one, from junior to senior. All others more or less supported my view except the Director (Finance). At that stage he closed the meeting and I came back to my room. Later, thinking about the process I realised why Mr. Rao had called me and why he had followed that particular sequence. If he had done it in the reverse order from senior to junior or at random it was likely that he may not have got the true opinion from the junior members.

I had my next experience of an effective decision making style immediately after I joined ICI India at the Kolkata Head Office as Head of Personnel/HR. Mr. Vijay Raghvan was the Managing Director. On the first Monday after my joining I got a call from his Secretary that there would be a meeting of the Management Committee at 11 a.m. followed by lunch. I came to know that the MD had started a practice of weekly meetings of his top team every Monday starting at 11 a.m. and then carried over with lunch at the Bengal Club next door. (In fact it was so close that we used to walk from ICI's office at 34 Chowringhee to Bengal Club through the narrow lane in between) In this meeting after a briefing by the MD on important issues, each one of us could raise any issue and get the decision which was largely arrived by consensus but failing the consensus the MD would give his ruling. No need for long notes or paperwork.

Sometimes the lightning speed of a decision can be surprising. When I was transferred from Kolkata to our explosives factory in Jharkhand at Gomia I was not eligible for a company car. Shortly after my transfer one day the Chief Executive of the Explosive Division Mr. Shiven Verma came to Gomia. Till late evening we were busy in the meeting. We came out of the office together and while walking towards our respective cars, Shiven noticed that I was heading towards a 'fiat' car. He asked me "OP you don't have a company car. Why? (Since all company cars were Ambassador Cars, it was obvious that I did not have a company car.) I said "Perhaps my salary may be below the eligibility requirement". He didn't say anything further. Next morning, as scheduled, he flew back to Kolkata in the company plane and I reached office. At around 9.30 a.m. our Admin Manager, Vasant Baliga walked into my office with a car key and a wireless from Shiven Verma saying "Give Company car to Khetan". I was happily surprised at the development and kept admiring the speed of decision making by Shiven Verma.

I learnt my next lesson on decision making while negotiating a long term agreement with an experienced Trade Union leader and President of our recognised Union, Mithlesh Kumar Sinha. He was an elderly person belonging to the socialist party and had worked with Dr. Ram Manaohar Lohia. I had a good relationship with him. When the long term agreement was due, Sinha dropped in at my house one day. During the discussion he asked me "Om Prakashji is bar kitna increase de rahe hain? (How much increase are you giving this time?) I told him laughingly "Mithelesh Babu you don't expect me to open my cards so early." He smiled and said "kam se kam saw rupaye to badhaenge na?" (Surely you will increase at least hundred rupees.) This was in 1980 when 100 rupees increase was considered good. I kept quiet. The meeting ended.

It took us almost one year and many meetings at local plant level, then at the level of Deputy Labour Commissioner at Bokaro Steel city and finally at the level of Labour Commissioner at Patna to arrive at the settlement. In between there were strike notices, walk outs from the meetings and all the drama associated with collective bargaining. It made negotiations all the trickier because there were two Unions and we had to negotiate the same terms with both the Unions who refused to sit together. Anyway, after considerable efforts of the saner elements on both sides an agreement was reached and signed at the level of Labour Commissioner. The total increase in monetary terms came to around hundred rupees!

After returning from Patna, I invited Sinha to my house to thank him for his constructive role. I also mentioned to him in all seriousness "Mithlesh Babu, we wasted so much time and money in travelling to Bokaro Steel City and Patna so many times. If I had accepted your offer that day, one year ago all this could have been saved. The old man paused for a while and then replied, and I will never forget his wise words backed by years of experience (He was much older than me). He said "Om Prakash ji, it was good that you did not commit anything that day. If you had accepted my offer and we had signed the agreement that day, neither I would have been able to satisfy my Union members nor would you have satisfied your management." He continued "The process of negotiation and hard bargaining that we went through for the last one year was necessary to provide satisfaction and acceptance on both the sides." How true and full of wisdom those words were. A decision which does not provide acceptance and satisfaction to the parties or persons concerned is not worth the paper on which it is recorded. The process of decision making is as important as the decision itself.

This was again proved recently at the political level when Rahul Gandhi, Vice President of Congress Party tore off the ordinance so as not to allow highly tainted politicians to take part in elections. The general feeling was that while the decision itself was not wrong the process was wrong. It would have been better if Rahul Gandhi had conveyed his views to the Prime Minister Dr. Manmohan Singh and the Prime Minister had announced the decision to withdraw the ordinance.

The lesson is: Three of the important requirements of an effective decision are quality, process and speed.

CHAPTER 13

Don't make a habit of criticizing & complaining

*"Any fool can criticize, condemn, and
complain and many fools do, but it
takes character and self-control to be
understanding and forgiving."*
Dale Carnegie

My first job after training in a steel plant in the US was as a Junior Engineer in the Machine Shop of Durgapur Steel Plant of SAIL. About 15 of my batch mates were also posted in various other sections of the Maintenance Department. We had a common boss - Superintendent of Maintenance. He was an old timer with the habit of scolding and criticising everyone for petty faults. Whenever any of our batch mates was called by him we used ask him on his return 'what happened? What did he say?' The common reply went like this "Are yaar bhagwan ne do kaan diye hai. Ek kaan se suna aur dosare se nikal diya. Ab kya bataun ki kya kaha". (Listen friend, God has given us two ears. I Listened from one and took out from the other. Now what should I tell you?) In effect the boss's communication, instruction and advice had no impact because the mode was not the right one. This is what normally happens in real life. If we want someone to listen to us we have to first make sure that he is willing to do so.

During my service period once I was transferred from Kolkata to a factory location. The house which I was to occupy was not vacant and I had to spend about three months in the guesthouse. Since this period coincided with the new school session I got my son Alok admitted in the school at the new location and he stayed with me in the guest house. Many senior officers on tour used to visit the factory frequently. When our guest house stay was about to end my son asked me one day "Daddy Mr. Complaint bahot din se nahi aye". (Daddy Mr. Complaint has not visited for a long time) I was completely taken aback by this remark of his. He hardly had any interaction with the person concerned except seeing him in the evening now and then. I realised from his remark how critically others are watching our behaviour.

In the 2014 election to the Indian Parliament contested by two major parties, Congress and BJP, there were high voltage canvassing, rallies and speeches. I am not aligned to any political party. But the media, electronic as well as print said that Mrs. Sonia Gandhi's one speech in which she called Narendra Modi as 'Maut Ka Saudagar'

(Merchant of death) went against the Congress Party. Similarly I remember that when V. P. Singh won the election and took over as Prime Minister defeating Rajiv Gandhi, in the first statement that he made to the nation he said, and I still remember the exact words, 'Sarkar ka khazana khali hai' (Government has no money) meaning that the previous Government has left the country's finance in disarray. The general feeling was that this was in bad taste and V. P. Singh did not get any political mileage out of it.

Why criticism and complaining is not the best way to get others to listen to you? Because it sets up a defence mechanism within them. The moment we start criticising and complaining the other person starts justifying his or her actions. During my service period and even during my training programmes many times one of the listeners would disagree with the proposal and when I would ask him OK what is your suggestion, there would be complete silence. Let us remember that unless we have a better idea we have no business to oppose or criticise the ideas and suggestions of others. This has happened so often with me that during the latter part of my career I made it a practice during my meetings that whenever anybody would criticise or disagree with the idea or suggestion of others, rather than arguing with him, I would ask him for his own suggestion. And if he gave a better suggestion, why not accept it? I have also experienced that people with high EQ don't criticise anything, they just give their own suggestions which has a better chance of acceptance.

Recently my granddaughter Akanksha was married to Robert, an Australian citizen at Dubai. I was asked to speak and give my blessings on the occasion. A grandfather is expected to give some advice for a happy married life. I thought about it for long. The advice had to be short, sweet and simple. Ultimately I opted for the four simple words. **"Never criticise your spouse".** In fact I am convinced that that if all the married couples follow these simple four words many marriages could be saved and many divorces would also not take place.

After retirement I have settled down in Gurgaon and live in one of the high rise buildings called Hamilton Court. We have a Condominium of three high rise buildings which include Windsor Court and Regency Park – II. I have been the President of the Residents' Welfare Association (RWA) as well as the President of the Condominium Association (CA). I learned more lessons about the havoc of criticism and complaining after retirement and after I have devoted myself to social service for the RWA and CA. During service if you are in a position of authority the occasion to face criticism and complaints are few and far between, more so if you are a good performer. But in a RWA each resident expresses his or her views freely. I have seen in our society that those residents who have a habit of criticising anything and everything slowly get isolated from the society. The Society stops paying any attention to their views and ultimate they are the sufferers.

Whenever we see unsatisfactory performance or behaviour around us it is very difficult to stop the temptation to take immediate action upon the person concerned. I understand that in the Defence Services there is a rule to handle such situations. The rule says, so I am told, that you have to sleep over it for a day and then on the next day if you still feel like taking the action go ahead. The sleeping over period of one day allows us to analyse the whole thing dispassionately and go by the verdict of the head rather than the heart.

By reading the above if you are getting the impression that I am debarring all criticism and complaints it is not so. If the situation really calls for corrective action please do so. But then let us remember that there is a right way and the right time. And also let us remember that unless we have a better suggestion, we have no business of criticising and complaining.

The lesson is: Avoid criticism as far as possible. Give suggestions instead.

CHAPTER 14

How to point out mistakes without offending

"Everyone makes mistakes, but admit your own before you point out someone else's"
Anonymous

The art of criticising without offending is so little known that the very word criticism leaves a bad taste in our mouth. However the real purpose should be not to beat the other person down or to hurt his feelings but to help him do better in future. The following real life experiences may help you to draw your own lessons.

In one of the factories where I was posted as General Manager (HR) an accident took place. The situation was tense and a circular had to be issued quickly. I dictated the circular to my secretary, made some corrections in the draft and asked him to retype it and issue it. Suddenly I realised that since it was an important piece of communication I should show it to my assistant. I called Kailash Singh my Industrial Relations Manager and asked him

"Kailash Singh just see this circular. Is it OK?"

He read it slowly and took more time than necessary, perhaps went over it twice and said

"Sir it looks OK. You must have written after thinking through."

By his body language and his taking so much time I could understand that there was something in his mind but it was not forthcoming. I asked him.

"Looks like there is something in your mind but you are not coming out."

"Sir nothing very important. I was only thinking that suppose instead of this sentence we write it like this then how will it look."

The moment he said it I realised that I was making a mistake and he was suggesting the correction.

I told him "Kailash thank you for pointing it out, why didn't you tell me immediately"

He replied "No Sir your idea was equally good. I have given my suggestion since you asked me"

In a nut shell he pointed out my mistake without offending me and letting me save my face. I have quoted the dialogue verbatim without even changing the name.

Another incident I remember took place during my conversation with Mr. Chaturanan Mishra. He was the national President of the AITUC Union and also President of our factory trade Union 'Gomia Mazdoor Sabha'. He was also a sitting MLA in the Bihar Assembly. Later he became the Cabinet Minister (Fertilizer & Chemicals) during United Front Government at the Centre. Once it so happened that five workers of our factory including a Vice President of that Union assaulted our Deputy Manager. We suspended them and started disciplinary action. In addition I also made a trip to Patna to meet Mr. Mishra. The news had already reached him. He was living in a MLA flat. I reached there accompanied by our Patna representative Vijay Topa. I thought the best way to deal with Mr. Mishra would be to be on the offensive. I started:

"Mishraji how do allow such people in your Union and make him Vice President, who assaults our managers?"

Mishraji saw my anger and heard me patiently. After I finished he asked me politely

"Om Prakashji did he become the Vice President of my Union before you recruited him as a worker in your factory".

I replied without giving much thought about what he meant.

"How is it relevant?"

He replied "Yours is a very reputed organisation with lots of resources. Before recruiting a worker you must have checked his antecedents and his background. Once you found a person good enough to be your worker we assumed that he was good enough to become our Union member. And as regards Vice Presidentship, ours is a democratic setup and any of our members can get elected to any position."

I had calmed down by then and my fast bowling had also slowed down. But I still persisted

"But Mishraji do you support your members including your Vice President assaulting our managers?"

He replied "No I don't support and I have already expressed my disapproval to them"

To summarise, Mishraji was pointing out my mistake without offending me. He was telling me that you people don't do your job of selecting your workers with due care and when they caused indiscipline you come here to blame me.

The third incident that I recollect also happened in one of our factories where I was working as General Manager

(Personnel and Admin.) Hari Kishore was my Admin Manager. He used to look after the canteen, security, transport, estate etc. It was my habit to make a round of one or two of my areas first thing in the morning when work started at 7.30 in the morning. That day I went straight to the canteen and found that the workers were following a particular procedure. I thought a different procedure would be better and asked them to change and came back. About an hour later Hari Kishore walked into my room and asked very politely:

"Sir did you go to the canteen this morning?" I said "yes".

He continued and his politeness also continued "Sir did you give such and such instructions?"

I again said "Yes, what happened?"

He replied "Sir yesterday I had given the opposite instruction because of such and such reasons and this morning I had to cut a sorry face."

I told Kishore that that was not my intention.

Then he said "Sir you are the boss. You can always overrule me. But can I make a request?"

"Yes Why not?"

"Sir in future if you give any instruction directly please let me know or the best thing would be either you take me along or ask me to give whatever instructions you want".

Needless to say, Kishore was pointing out my mistake without offending me. I told Kishore that in future he would have no problem.

Later when I started HRD Centre and was conducting training programmes in the leading hotels in Delhi such as Maurya Sheraton, Taj Palace and Marriot etc. on occasions when the service was not up to the mark I found a neat way of pointing out the deficiency without offending the person concerned. I would say that the quality of a particular dish was not befitting the standard of Maurya Sheraton or that the conference room Layout was not befitting the name of Marriot Hotel or something similar. And invariably I found that this was more acceptable as it boosted their ego.

To sum up, I suggest the following guidelines for pointing out mistakes without offending.

- **Give a face saver**
- **Point out the mistake indirectly**
- **Suggest an alternative**
- **Boost the ego**

CHAPTER 15

What's in a name

"That which we call a rose by any other name would smell as sweet".
William Shakespeare,
Romeo and Juliet

A person's name is the sweetest and most important sound to him or her. My first experience of what's in a name took place after I joined Hindustan Steel Ltd., the earlier incarnation of Steel Authority of India Ltd. (SAIL) as a Graduate Apprentice. We used to hear that Mr. Sukhu Sen who was the plant head at the Bhilai Steel Plant and was later elevated to the position of General Manager was an expert steel technologist. When he was recruited he was to fill an application form. I heard that in the qualification column he only wrote 'Sukhu Sen' and in spite of further enquiries, the Government of India could not elicit any further details. I heard that he was so experienced that he could tell the composition of steel by seeing the colour of the flame inside the steel melting furnace through the peep hole. So you know what's in a name.

One habit of Sukhu Sen made him dear to the hearts of the lowest grade of workers called 'Khalasi' in the steel language. Sukhu Sen would only smoke a bidi, not a cigarette. Sometimes under pressure or tension he would light a bidi and have a few puffs even inside the plant. At that time if a worker was around he would offer the bidi to him also, though out of regard or fear no one would normally accept. But sometimes when his own stock was over he would go and ask the nearest known bidi smoker for a bidi. This habit of his was the talk of the plant. The worker whom he asked for the bidi would tell others with untold pride "Aaj bade sahib ne hamse bidi mangi" (today the big boss asked me for a bidi). This reminded me of one of the requirements of a leader which I read long ago. "A leader must be perceived as one of us". The other two requirements are "A leader must be perceived as the best of us" and "A leader must be perceived as most of us".

My next experience took place when I was working as Chief of Personnel at Rourkela Steel Plant of SAIL. Mr. Mohan Kumar Mangalam was the Steel Minister. First time when he visited the plant I was introduced to him. I was also present in the meeting for performance review along with other top managers. Next time when the Minister visited Rourkela there was no need for reintroduction. But I wasn't so sure. So I tried to introduce myself again but before I could speak the Minister said "Yes of course I know you Khetan". I really got a kick out of it thinking that the Minister remembered my name amongst so many managers he must have met last time.

The most learning experience happened when I was posted to the explosives factory of ICI (now taken over by Orica) at Gomia located in Jharkhand. One day the Deputy Labour Commissioner Sharda Nandan Singh visited the factory and wanted to meet the Union leaders. So I organised a meeting of about half a dozen workers who were prominent Union leaders. I was new to the plant and knew the names of a few of them. But I was surprised when Sharda Babu (this is how I addressed him) greeted each one of them by name. They were extremely happy to see that a Govt Official knew them by name. They all paid him high regard and a few younger ones even touched his feet. Although our factory was important, Sharda Babu used to visit many factories in the region. To see him remembering the names of all our Union leaders was a lesson I never forgot.

After I joined ICI India whenever a visitor came from ICI U.K. a drill was followed. He would be sent a list of names along with the photographs of all the managers he was likely to meet at the site and he was expected to practice and remember all the names by recognising the face. The net result was that when he visited India and met you for the first time he could address you by name. This made a lasting impression on the person concerned by giving him a feeling of importance

When I was posted at the Head Office of ICI India at Kolkata I used to visit our Hyderabad factory at Balanagar. This was a paints factory and Raj Verma, one of our top class managers, was posted as the Factory Manager. It had around 100 workers and supervisors. During my first visit he took me around the factory. I saw him addressing each one of the workers by name and the more surprising thing was that in most cases he knew the names of their family members too. While talking he would first enquire about the family. If anybody was sick in the family or if there was any problem of school admission of children or housing loan etc. Then he would come to performance. No wonder the productivity of our Hyderabad factory was always high.

One of the most important events about what's in a name took place during the merger of Mittal steel and Arcelor S.A. The story goes that after hard negotiations lasting over several days and several meetings the last hitch was about the name. I understand that Arcelor wanted that their name should come first in the combined name and that is how the merged company was called ArcelorMittal. So you know what's in a name.

Why go that far? Let us have a look at our daily lives. Why do we go after brand names for our daily utilities even though it may cost us much more? And why does the whole advertising business keep popularising brand names? Obviously names and brand names are important, very important.

But most of us, while we give importance to brand names, hardly give any importance to human names. It is commonly seen that after getting introduced to a stranger and after chatting with him for a few minutes we don't remember his name when we say goodbye. Why not make a little effort and start a new practice from tomorrow. Let us try to remember the names of all those we meet and come in contact in future. This will be the easiest way to make people like us and we can do it in business as well as in social life.

The lesson is: A person's name is the most important sound to him. Let us try to remember the names of all those we meet.

CHAPTER 16

Mind your manners

"Good manners will open doors that the best education cannot."
Clarence Thomas

Manners, etiquette and behaviour show our consideration for others. These are alternate names for kindness, tact and respect. In some people these are inborn but in many of us these are to be inculcated. Good manners oil the wheels of our daily contact with other human beings, thereby reducing friction. Success in work life as well as social life depends as much on our good manners as on the knowledge and skill of the subject. This is true whether we are attending a job interview, a sales call, a presentation or joining a social meet. The following real life incidents provide some dos and don'ts.

One day I was in my office at Kolkata. One of our newly recruited management trainees, Rakesh (name changed) walked in. As HR Head of the company I was his mentor. After a couple of months we had become quite close as I was spending an hour or so with him every week to guide him and solve his problems if any. He said "Sir I have learned a lot in this company". I was curious. He continued "Yesterday I was invited for lunch by the big boss, the CEO of my business. All the departmental managers were there. I had never been to such a grand party. So I joined the queue and when my turn came I filled up my plate with chicken and rice and all the other delicacies and started enjoying the delicious food. Mr. Sharan Vir Singh (He was the business CEO) who was on the other side of the table slowly started moving towards me but on the way casually talking with others. He came to my side and almost whispered in my ears in such a way that no one else could hear. "Young man I know that you are hungry and the food is delicious. But why fill the plate at one time. Why not take a little, finish it and then take a second helping and if you still feel like, take the third helping. Isn't that better?" While saying so he quietly and casually moved away. In those few minutes I had learned a lesson about table manners which I will remember throughout my life".

I am surprised to find that even at an advanced age people have not learned these basic manners. Currently we have a Senior Citizen's Council at Gurgaon. They have organised group tours in India and abroad. In these tours buffet meals are laid out and there is a wide choice. I find some people in the group still behave the same way as Rakesh did many years ago. Subtle hints have not worked so far.

I am also surprised to find the lack of etiquettes even among senior citizens whenever the Council organises an evening programme followed by buffet dinner. Some of them will keep talking either among themselves or on the mobile phone even when the proceedings are going on. Not realising that it disturbs others and not even aware that they are being branded as uncivilised.

Another incident which I remember took place during the early part of my career. In those days I was working as a Junior Officer at the head Office of Hindustan Steel Ltd. (SAIL) at Ranchi. The Management Training Institute (MTI) of the company was also located at Ranchi. Mr. Shreenagesh ICS, was the chairman of HSL/SAIL. After the inauguration of a new training programme, the head of MTI was to accompany the Chairman in the car. The driver had parked the car in such a way that the chairman would sit on the back seat on the other side of the driver's seat. The Chairman went in and sat down on his usual seat. The MTI Head was expected to move to the other side and sit from that side. But he was not well versed with the manners and etiquette. He kept waiting on the same sided expecting the Chairman to shift to the other side. We were all watching the scene. After a few minutes the Chairman must have realised what was happening. He quietly asked the MTI Head to come from the other side. This one incident remained the talking point in the organisation for a long time and brought down the image of the person.

One incident of lack of etiquette on the part of one of my junior colleagues caused lot of embarrassment to me. I had invited a Govt. Official and his wife for dinner at a five star hotel in Delhi. My wife joined me and I had asked one of my assistants Gaurav (name changed) who was a bachelor, also to join in. He was a non-vegetarian. Rest of us were vegetarians. The dinner was ordered. Somehow the rice and the non-vegetarian dishes arrived earlier. Gaurav started serving the rice and non-veg dishes on his plate and when he saw that the vegetarian dishes were taking time he started eating. I gave him a disapproving look but perhaps he was not sensitive enough to understand. Later when I pointed this out to him he realised that he should not have done it.

The last episode which I would like to quote relates to the etiquette followed by my boss Thampi, who later became Chairman of BASF India, a German multinational. He would always follow a practice that he must have imbibed in his early life. Whenever I would visit his house and when I would be driving the car he would open and close the door for my wife to get out and get in comfortably.

These actions or inactions appear small but they leave a lasting impression on others. Others can't see your knowledge or money but they can see your behaviour and manners.

The lessons are that good manners, etiquettes and behaviour are necessary if you want to create a good impression on others and get accepted and respected in civilised society.

CHAPTER 17

Win-win solution is possible

"Unless both sides win,
no solution can be permanent."
Jimmy Carter

I had read about it in my management lessons but wasn't sure if it worked in practice. In one of the professional conferences at Kanpur, one of my colleagues, Suresh Saxena, told me his recent experience of resolving a problem which could easily fit into this. I am quoting below what Saxena told me:

One day Lalaji (big boss) gave me an urgent call to come to his office immediately. When I reached there, Lalaji was spitting fire. He told me "Saxena who recruited this Nand Kishore (NK). I don't want to see his face. Fire him immediately". Nand Kishore was a bright young man recruited as a management trainee and had been confirmed recently. Even Lalaji used to like him but something must have upset Lalaji. Mustering some courage I told him "But Lalaji how can we fire him. We have taken him from one of the Indian Institutes of Management and have recently confirmed him". Lalaji lost no time in replying "Fir Aapko kis liye rakha hai." (Then why have I employed you?) I understood his meaning, assured Lalaji that he would not see him again and came back to my room.

I called Nand Kishore and asked him what had happened and why Lalaji was so upset. What Nand Kishore told me was that he wanted to introduce a new performance management system so that there was a rational system of deciding increments in future but Lalaji did not want any such system. He was happy in deciding increments by himself. When Nand Kishore asserted and insisted, Lalaji got furious and asked him to get out and called Saxena.

After hearing NK I asked him to proceed on a month's leave and go for a honeymoon. "But Sir I have already had my honeymoon six months back". NK replied. I told him "Have your second honeymoon or whatever, but don't come to the office from tomorrow. Keep in touch with me and I will tell you what to do next".

After an hour or so when I went to Lalaji he asked me "Nand Kishore gaya?" (Has NK gone?) I told him "yes". Lalaji was satisfied and we talked about other things. Back in his office Saxena started thinking about the 'win-win' solution which we used to discuss in our professional discussions.

After a week or so there was an industrial relations problem. The Union leaders of one of the unrecognised Union wanted to see Lalaji. NK had won their confidence and used to accompany them and manage them in such meetings. Lalaji was apprehensive and asked Saxena to replicate Nand Kishore. Saxena said he would try his best and added in a soft voice "I will try to locate Nand Kishore just for this meeting" Lalaji did not say yes or no. Since Saxena was close to the rival recognised Union, he could not manage the situation as well as NK. Lalaji was upset but kept quiet.

After a week there was an invitation from the local Chamber of Commerce of which Lalaji was the President and had to deliver the Presidential address. On earlier occasions NK, being a qualified MBA, had been his speech writer. Saxena was no match for this. Anyway, Lalaji called Saxena and wanted his suggestion. Saxena said "I will call NK for a day and ask him to write the speech". Lalaji was relieved and avoided further details. NK came to the office wrote the speech, did some other pending work and left.

After two weeks there was an accident in the factory. One contract labour died due to electrocution since the contractor was not using the safety equipment. There was commotion in the factory. Workers wanted to Gherao Lalaji. But since Lalaji was alerted by his Security Officer he did not come to the factory. Saxena was holding the fort. He knew that a batch mate of NK had been posted as SDM at Kanpur. Nevertheless to be sure Saxena rang NK but found that the news had already reached NK through his intelligence system and NK had already contacted the SDM who had assured all help. In the meantime Lalaji was a worried man. He rang Saxena and asked him to do whatever but that there should be no labour problem. Saxena was just waiting for this day. He told Lalaji about NK's contact with the SDM. He also told Lalaji that NK had not joined any other organisation so far and could be asked to re-join. Lalaji kept quiet. Saxena got the message. He rang NK and told him "Your honeymoon leave is over. Come to the office immediately and join duty."

This is a real life story told to me by Saxena. Alas he is no more. But the simple win-win solution adopted by him will always remain in my memory. For obvious reasons I have not disclosed the name of the organisation.

My next experience with a win-win solution took place during the year 2001 when Maruti wanted to implement its first voluntary retirement scheme (VRS). I got a call from Sudhakar their Head of Human Resources who knew me from Steel Authority days when both of us were working at Rourkela Steel Plant. Maruti had prepared a first class VRS. All they wanted me to do was to sell it to their departmental heads. The day was 19th September 2001. About 40 departmental heads participated in a daylong meeting with me. We jointly explored the possibility of win-win solutions. While Maruti was interested in rationalizing its manpower we felt that some of the employees would be interested in their hard pressed need for money. Such needs were identified as marrying their daughter or sister, starting a business or joining a business with a family member or a friend. The employees nearing retirement would like to settle down in their home town and would need money to buy or build a house. It was agreed that such win-win solutions were possible and should be fully explored. The senior operating officials took up the ownership and the VRS was a success.

My next experience took place during collective bargaining with the CITU Trade Union at our Kanpur Fertilizer plant of Indian Explosives. I was heading the negotiations from the management's side. The main issues about wage and other benefits had been settled and the agreement was ready for signing but the Union leader Arvind Kumar confided in me that one of his shop representatives from the laboratory was coming in the way. He wanted that their various problems should be resolved speedily. On the other hand the departmental head wanted that the test frequency should be increased. I thought these matters could be settled at the dept level and did not want to waste time. Suddenly one of my bright team mates Aditya Narayan asked me whether he could try. I said go ahead. He took both the Department Head and the Union Representative aside, discussed with them and brought the following draft for my approval. "The management agrees to look into all the grievances of the laboratory staff speedily. The Union agrees that all efforts will be made to increase the frequency of tests". Both sides agreed and the agreement was signed. Aditya Narayan later became the Chairman of the company at a young age.

The last win-win solution that I want to mention here happened when I was working as HR Head of Indian Explosive's Fertilizer Division and was posted at Delhi. My office was at Hindustan Times House, Kasturba Gandhi Marg near Connaught Place. Management was offering voluntary retirement scheme (VRS) to staff. One day my assistant Rajan Singhal came to me and said that that one of the staff members was willing to opt for VRS but had a peculiar problem. He was not getting along with his wife and didn't have a comfortable house. Here in the office he spent the entire day in air conditioned comfort with free tea/coffee. So even though he was interested in VRS he didn't want to spend the whole day at home. We thought over the matter and found a neat solution. We made him a member of the library at the American Centre on the KG Marg. There he could read newspapers and books of his choice and spend the whole day in the most comfortable environment. He readily agreed and accepted VRS. A win-win solution was found

The lesson is: A win-win solution is possible in most cases if we try really hard.

CHAPTER 18

How to handle a crisis

*"When written in Chinese, the word 'crisis'
is composed of two characters.
One represents danger and the other
represents opportunity"*
John F. Kennedy

It is difficult to lay down any concrete rules or procedures for handling a crisis. In most cases the presence of mind and past experience comes in handy. However I am quoting below a few of my real life experiences in the hope that these may give you some ideas and guidance.

The first incident happened when I was working as head of Personnel at Indian Explosives' Fertilizer Plant at Kanpur. One day during lunch time, suddenly I heard a big commotion as if many workers had collected outside my office. My Secretary rushed to my room and said that a large number of workers with a lunch tray wanted to force their entry into my room. I tried to compose myself and asked her to open the door. In came the Union President followed by other Executive members and a large number of workers. My office was full to the brim and the workers occupied the corridor also. Along with them the Canteen Manager also entered the room.

The Union President showed me a black thing in the dal and said they had been complaining of the bad food quality in the past but so far it had fallen on deaf ears of the management. Today they had got solid proof of a cockroach in the dal and they wanted action by the management. I was thinking of how to save the situation. Suddenly I saw the Canteen Manager (CM) taking out the black thing from the dal and putting it in his mouth and saying "where is the cockroach? This is Badi Elaichi". (Black cardamom) While saying so he gulped it down his throat and there was no trace of it in his mouth. I was amazed to see all this. The Union President and workers were nonplussed but furious. They knew that their proof had disappeared. They started calling names to the CM. But the CM kept his cool and kept on insisting that it was only a piece of Badi Elaichi otherwise how could he put it in the mouth. Anyway I got the opening which I was looking for and somehow managed the situation with the assurance of improving the food quality in future. As regards the cockroach the truth never came out because later whenever I asked the CM he would insist that it was a Badi Elaichi although my own feeling was that it was a cockroach!

The next incident happened when I was working as the Head of Human Resource Management at Rourkela Steel Plant (RSP). One morning as soon I reached office I got an SOS from the Deputy General Manager in charge of Admin Mr. L. I. Parija I.A.S. (he later became Chief Secretary, Orissa) to come to his room immediately. When I reached there, he informed me that the General Manager (GM) was on the line and he was very furious. He wanted my Private Secretary to be suspended immediately. On further inquiry, Parija quickly told me the following story. RSP had a small plane for VIP duties which used to fly between Rourkela and Kolkata. Being a Public Sector company, it was also used by workers on medical emergencies. That morning, the GM was to travel from Rourkela to Kolkata for onward journey to Delhi. However when the plane flew from Kolkata to Rourkela in the morning it was used by someone who was unwell and he had vomited in the plane. Normally a sweeper was on duty at the airport whenever the plane was due to land and take off; but that day he was absent without notice. So when the GM wanted to board the plane the pilot told him to wait for the cleaning. But there was no sweeper around. The GM was upset with the delay because he had an appointment with the Steel Minister that day at Delhi and could not afford to miss the Kolkata Delhi flight. He rang up the DGM. The PS to DGM asked him about his identity and why he wanted to talk. The GM was upset by the questions and rather than wasting time in answering these questions he again asked him in a stern voice to connect immediately. However the PS still didn't realise who the caller was and insisted on the identity. It is at that point that the GM lost his cool and told him who he was and also asked the DGM to suspend the PS immediately for being rude to him and not recognising his voice. We discussed the matter and decided to tell the GM that yes we would suspend the PS because it appeared the GM was in no mood to listen.

We verbally counselled and cautioned the PS and told him to use his common sense to apply the rules with discretion. When the GM came back from Delhi we met him with a back dated suspension letter and told him that we had prepared the letter as instructed by him and were ready to issue it but felt that the case called for a review by him. By that time the GM had forgotten the whole incident and told us to do whatever we thought right.

The next crisis also happened at Rourkela Steel Plant (RSP). The plant had an elaborate system of joint committees representing management as well as the workers nominated by the Recognised Union. The total membership was around 800. The steel Secretary Wadud Khan who was also the first Chairman of SAIL was visiting RSP and it was decided to organise a function of the joint committees in the plant auditorium known as Gopbandhu Auditorium with a seating capacity of around 1000. On the fateful day the hall was packed to capacity with Executives and workers occupying all the seats. On the dais were the Steel Secretary cum Chairman SAIL, the GM, the DGM and myself. I started the function by extending a hearty welcomed to everyone and then requested the GM to address the gathering. Suddenly I saw the President of the recognised Union along with a couple of his lieutenants entering the auditorium and not finding any empty chairs, sat down on the floor in the well of the auditorium in front of the dais. I could see the tension among workers in the audience due to this and was thinking what to do. Suddenly I got an idea. I got down from the dais, went where the Union President was sitting and sat by his side on the floor. My deputy S. S. Parida also did the same. I could immediately feel the tension in the hall melting down. After sitting for some time on the floor, when my turn came to speak again, I went up the dais.

The next and the last crisis which I want to mention happened with me a few years ago. The day was normal. Around nine in the evening my wife started breathing heavily. I thought of calling a doctor in the campus. I rang up my son who was living next door. He and his wife came within five minutes. In the meantime my wife's condition grew worse. She was unable to breathe. While I was dithering, my son decided to immediately shift her to the Max Hospital nearby. He said "Daddy I am bringing the car near the lift, bring Mummy down" In the meantime my wife fainted. But helped by my daughter-in-law, we carried her to the car and my son drove the car to the Max Hospital, Gurgaon, and reached there within ten minutes. As soon as the car stopped at emergency, Doctor Murty and his staff were ready with a stretcher even without our informing them. Perhaps this was their drill. Hats off to Dr. Murty and Max Hospital. My wife was taken to a bed and emergency treatment started. To cut the long story short she was diagnosed with a blockage in one of the arteries and a stent was put. The learning point is that the quick decision taken by my son to shift her to the hospital immediately may have saved her life.

To sum up, the lessons are: Handling a crisis requires presence of mind, quick decision making, out of box solutions and plenty of common sense.

CHAPTER 19

Why some people succeed while others fail

*"The will to win, the desire to succeed,
the urge to reach your full potential...
These are the keys that will unlock the door
to personal excellence."*
Confucius

From time immemorial behavioural scientists have been conducting research on "what makes us successful and star performers?" Is it luck alone? Or intelligence? Or personality? Or something else? And whatever it is inborn or can it be acquired, nurtured or developed by care, training and practice? Why all the gold medallists and toppers from schools, colleges and universities are not always the toppers in real life? Are there some other factors which have a higher degree of correlation with achievement and success?

The early notion that what matters for success is IQ alone was not borne out by the facts when it was found that many gold medallists were not always star performers while many people with average IQ had done better than toppers – why? The search continued.

Around 40 years ago Daniel Goleman of USA carried out research with the guidance of Prof. David McClelland, a Harvard Professor. He found that a package of human traits was a greater predictor of achievement and success than intelligence. He named this package as emotional intelligence (EQ). What is even more important for us is the fact that while IQ is inborn, EQ can be acquired and developed like any other skill? It has also been found that the importance of EQ increases the higher one goes up in the hierarchy.

The package of human traits named as EQ consists of:

Self-awareness
Self-regulation
Self-motivation
Social awareness and
Social skills

A study conducted by dozens of experts in about five hundred corporations over two years worldwide arrived independently at similar conclusions that EQ plays a major role in achieving excellence in any job. These ideas are not new. What is new is the data we now have of 25 years' worth of empirical studies with a previously unknown precision of just how much emotional intelligence matters for success.

Let us be clear of some misconceptions in people's mind about emotional intelligence (EQ):

Emotional Intelligence does not mean merely "being nice". At strategic moments it may demand "not being nice"

Secondly, EQ does not mean giving free rein to feelings "letting it all hang out". Rather it means managing feelings.

Women are not smarter than men are. Nor are men superior to women.

Finally, our level of EQ is not fixed genetically, nor does it develop only in early childhood unlike IQ which changes little after the teen years. EQ seems to be largely learned and it continues to develop as we go through life and learn from our experiences. This growth in EQ can be called maturity.

Our emotional intelligence determines our potential for acquiring emotional competence which results in outstanding performance. Simply being high in emotional intelligence does not guarantee that a person would have learned the emotional competencies that matter in performance: it only means that he has an excellent potential to learn them.

An intuitive decision is nothing but a subconscious analysis – somehow the brain goes through the churning process of these calculations and comes up with what we would call a weighted conclusion – it seem more right to do it this way than that way

The importance of human characteristics included in the EQ package is borne out by the fact that a comprehensive study of what the leading corporations were seeking in MBAs mentioned the following as the most desirable capabilities:

Communication skills
Interpersonal skills
Initiative

In my in-house management training programmes, I have been conducting a very interesting exercise by asking the participants to rate each other and also rate themselves on various factors. We have found that in most cases the rating of a person about himself/herself differs from the one given by others. Which brings us to the two important characteristics in the package of EQ i.e. self-awareness and social awareness.

How to increase our self-awareness and social awareness? Two behavioural scientists have found a systematic way called "Johari window" to do so. In simple terms it requires us to keep our feedback channels unclogged. When someone gives us feedback about us, our behaviour, our attitudes, our manners, such as getting angry too often, talking too much or too little, being negative most of the time and so on, let us listen to the feedback. It is not very often that it happens. Normally people avoid giving such a feedback, so if somebody is doing it let us listen. He may have his own agenda and then we may disregard the feedback, but for God's sake let us listen. In fact if we want to increase our self-awareness and social awareness we must take the initiative to invite such a feedback from our trusted family members and friends.

Once we know the areas which require changes and improving, we could take these up one by one and prepare a time bound action plan with mileposts to improve these areas and thus improve our Emotional Competence (EQ).

The lesson is: If we want to achieve success in life and want to become star performers let us try to improve our emotional competence.

CHAPTER 20

How to motivate ourselves

*"Arise! Awake! and stop not
until the goal is reached."*
Swami Vivekananda

In the earlier chapters we have discussed 'how to motivate people' and 'how to motivate the team'. What is equally important or perhaps even more is 'how to motivate ourselves?' I have learnt from experience that **the very first requirement is to avoid the company of de-motivators.** When I was studying for my M.Tech. at IIT Kharagpur, I had a roommate. He had a negative attitude. I was preparing for the Engineering Services examination of UPSC. He would often discourage me saying that it was beyond me. Ultimately when I cleared the written examination and got the interview call he was surprised and rationalised it on luck. From the early days I realised that there was no point in arguing with him. So I started avoiding discussion on this topic. You will come across such people in your friends, colleagues and even relatives. Best thing is to avoid their company and ignore their comments.

The second requirement is to get rid of excuses such as

'I am too young'
'I am too old'
'I haven't had the right education'
'I didn't go to the right schools'
'I don't have the right family background'
'I suffer from poor health'
'I am not lucky'
'I was born under a wrong birth sign'

Let us take some examples. Narendra Modi neither went to the right schools; neither had the right education nor had the right family background while Manmohan Singh went to the best schools and had the best education. Who would you consider successful? I leave it to you. Or take another example - Rahul Gandhi had the right family background in fact the best family background. Did it help him? You decide.

Alexander the great died at the age of 32, Adi Shankaracharya and Swami Vivekanand both died when they were only 39 - so are you too young?

And if you think you are too old read this. Theodor Mommsen received the Noble Prize for literature at the age of 85. The American composer Elliot Carter, not content with writing his first opera at 90, published over 40 more works before he was 100 and was still working when he died at 103. Fauja Singh, a British national of Indian origin, entered the record books when he became the oldest person to complete a marathon at the age of 100. This was his eighth marathon; he ran his first one when he was 89. So are you too old?

The third requirement for motivating yourself is, don't fear failure. Many great men have tasted failure before their success including Henry Ford, Albert Einstein and Abraham Lincoln. According to Mahabharat, the Indian epic, Jarasandh the king of Magadh attacked Mathura 17 times in spite of getting defeated every time at the hands of Lord Krishna, but ultimately forced him to shift the capital from Mathura to Dwarka. And finally you must have read or heard the story of Robert Bruce the King of Scotland and the spider. So if you have failed so far, you are in good company and success is awaiting you.

The fourth requirement is that appearance builds confidence. Well begun is half done is the famous adage. The first thing others judge you by is your appearance. IBM always insisted that their salesmen should groom well, dress well and appear immaculately when they visited clients. First impression is the last impression whether meeting clients, appearing in an interview, speaking in public or on your first date.

The fifth requirement to motivate ourselves is compiling our records of past successes. Udit Shanker

Mathur, one of my son's friends had cleared the written examination and was to appear for the interview in S P Jain Institute of Management, Mumbai. He came to me for some tips. I asked him whether he had played any leadership role in the past. First he couldn't think of any. Then it occurred to him that he was the mess secretary at BITS Pilani during his Chem. Engineering Course. So I told him that that at his age no one expected him to be a political leader or an MLA or MP. The mess secretary ship was certainly a leadership role. He talked about it confidently in the interview and was selected. I can't say how much this reply played its part.

The sixth requirement for motivating us is assertiveness. After completing my M.Tech from IIT Kharagpur I appeared in the interview by Union Public Service Commission at Dholpur House, New Delhi for the post of Management Trainee in the Public Sector Steel Plants. During the interview one of the UPSC members asked me about the practical training which I had taken in the U. P. Govt. Roadways workshop at Kanpur. He asked me how the engine valve grinding was done. I told him the process and also added that I had done it manually. Perhaps he wanted to test me and told me that according to his information it was done mechanically and not manually. I got somewhat upset and told him assertively that "Sir, I have already told you that in the workshop where I took training it was done manually and I have done it with my own hands so why are you asking me again." Hearing this, the Chairman intervened and told me "OK Khetan you can go. Thank you". I came out with a heavy heart and told some of my batch mates waiting outside that I had spoilt my interview for no rhyme or reason but they cheered me and assured me of success. A month later I received the appointment letter to join.

And finally there is a Sanskrit shloka from Hitopadesha. The English translation of that shloka is:

There are three types of people in this world;

Lowest category:	Those who will not take up any project due to fear of difficulties or failure.
Middle category:	Those who will start the project but give up at the earliest difficulties.
Highest category:	Those who once start a project keep working at it in spite of all the difficulties and make a success of it

I am sure we all want to be in the highest category.

The lesson is: If we want to motivate ourselves let us remember and follow the above six requirements and success is awaiting us.

CHAPTER 21

How to handle complaints and grievances

"Kind words can be short and easy to speak,
but their echoes are truly endless."
Mother Teresa

One of the most important requirements for handling a complaint or a grievance is to listen patiently without interrupting the aggrieved person. After all, if we don't interrupt him or her how long can the person continue? One hour, no way, half an hour also no way, even fifteen minutes is not possible. The maximum time is more likely to be around five to seven minutes. Is it too long? During this period, we should not only listen but what is even more important is that the other person must feel that we have listened to and understood their problem and grievance. Even such a patient listening gives considerable satisfaction to the aggrieved person.

But what happens when we don't listen. I had this bitter experience and always felt sorry about it. This happened when I was working as the HR Head at one of the factories. One day I was sitting in my office and a worker named Raju walked in. He started narrating his problem. He had barely started when my telephone rang. Sheshadri the Deputy Production Manager was on the other side. He wanted to know the progress of recruitment for the new plant. It took me about five minutes to appraise him. I kept the telephone down and asked Raju to continue. Again after a few minutes my Secretary walked in to get some urgent papers signed. Once this was over I asked Raju to restart. He barely started when my Secretary walked in again and said that the other managers were waiting for me for the weekly 4 o'clock meeting. I saw the watch. It was five minutes past four. I got up from the chair and told Raju. "Achha Raju maine sun liya. Ab main dekhta hun kya ho sakta hai". (OK Raju I have heard your problem. Let me see what can be done). He said with sarcasm visible in his eyes. "Sir aapne to mujhe suna tak nahi. Aap to telephone aur papers mein lahe rahe meri problem kya solve karenge". (Sir you have not even listened to me, you were busy with the telephone and papers. How will you solve my problem?) After saying so he folded his hand and said Namaste and walked out of my room. Raju's response was very painful but it taught me an important lesson.

My boss, Russi Billimoria, used to tell me that once TATA Steel asked the renowned consultancy organisation McKenzie to carry out a management consultancy study.

One of the points of the study was to find out what gave the workers the highest degree of satisfaction. To the surprise of many, the workers rated the grievance handling system of Tata Steel as giving them the highest degree of satisfaction. No wonder people say that Russi Modi, the famous Ex Chairman of Tata Steel, used to follow an open door policy. Any worker or staff, if he was not satisfied, could walk into his room and present his or her grievance. But the risk was that if Russi Modi said 'NO', no one could change that decision come what may, so very few people took the risk.

It is common to face complaints whether in business or social life. And my experience says that the complaints provide us an opportunity to improve ourselves and our systems. In this connection I recollect my experience when I was working as the Head of the Human Resource at Rourkela Steel Plant. The plant had a work force of over 30,000 employees including about 2,000 Executives and Managers. After joining I was invited to the farewell function of a retiring employee. I asked him the usual questions about how he was feeling that day after the long service career. He told me that now that he had retired the most difficult part would be to get the last dues for which he would have to move from pillar to post. After the function was over I told my officers that in future I would like to hand over the last dues payment cheque to the retiring employees during the function. They all agreed that it was worth doing but pointed out many problems with respect to finance, Town Administration's Estate Wing and other departments, where clearance was required. We sorted out all these problems within the next three months and after that the cheque for the last dues was handed over in the farewell function to the retiring employee. The learning point is that the complaint helped in improving the procedure of payment of legitimate dues of a retiring employee.

For the last five years I am devoting time to social work and as a result have been elected as President of the Residents' Welfare Association or as a committee member. Many residents and staff take up their minor problems with me such as seepage of water from the floor above, too much noise from the top or bottom flat, staff not getting their salary in time from the contractors and a host of other issues. I find that if I listen to them patiently and try to understand the problem, half the satisfaction is assured. In addition if I involve them in the solution identification by asking their suggestion, it results in more satisfaction. And finally, if I involve them in implementing the solution it further improves the satisfaction level.

Is there any ideal way to handle complaints? Yes, there is, and social scientists have suggested the following procedure and sequence. My experience also says that if we follow these steps there is a good chance of success.

<u>Seven steps of Grievance handling</u>

1. Listen patiently as mentioned in the beginning even though this is the most difficult part.

2. Pay undivided attention – Avoid distractions like telephone calls, checking SMS/e-mail etc.

3. Let the person finish – Please avoid the temptation to interrupt

4. Show concern –"Yes I can understand your problem". "Yes I know how you must be feeling". "Yes If I were you I would feel similarly" etc.

5. Seek more information or clarification after the person has completed.

6. Be clear about the real problem.

7. If you can solve the problem do so then and there or else show empathy and give an appropriate reply and take the necessary action

CHAPTER 22

How to develop a positive attitude

*"Attitude is a little thing that
makes a big difference."*
Winston Churchill

My favourite story, although not a real life incident, which
I have often used in my management training programmes
goes like this. Once Bata Shoe Company sent two of
its Marketing Managers, Mahesh and Rakesh to the
interior of Africa to explore the market for its shoes in two
different territories. After extensive survey Mahesh sent
the message "No market for Bata Shoes because nobody
wears shoes here." However Rakesh sent a completely
different message "Good opportunity for Bata Shoes as
no other shoe maker has started operations here and we
will get the first mover advantage". If both Mahesh and
Rakesh are posted there who do you think is more likely

to succeed and why? Well the chances are that both may fail or both may succeed. But in a borderline scenario, Mahesh will have a better chance? Why? Although both are likely to face tremendous difficulties, but Mahesh will have a readymade excuse. He would justify his failure by rationalising that he had already given such a feedback. While it is a matter of losing face for Rakesh. He will move heaven and earth to succeed.

During my early service period it was common to hear from my colleagues "Yaar yeh boss suntan hi nahi hai. Uske paas time hi nahi hai". (This boss doesn't listen. He has no time for me.) These comments mellowed down as I moved up in the hierarchy. But the real analysis started during my management training programmes. I would raise the following question for discussion.

"The problem is not that the boss doesn't listen to you but your inability to choose the right time and his right mood."

The participants start thinking and discussing. A debate starts. Arguments and counter arguments follow. Some agree and some disagree. But everybody starts thinking that maybe they also need to change their attitude.

In fact we have a full session on how to develop a positive attitude in our management training programmes and the exercise which I found most effective and convincing is reproduced below:

Most people would agree that you get more from life when you think positively than when you think negatively. Positive people use the word **'and'** whereas negative people are more likely to use **'but'**. Here are some examples from the **'BUT BRIGADE'.**

1. I would like to put forward more ideas in the company **but** my boss will probably not have time to listen to them.

2. I would like to offer better quality product to my customers **but** if I raise the price they will probably think that I am squeezing more money out of them.

3. I would like to suggest some changes in our society to improve the quality of life **but** the committee is unlikely to pay heed.

4. I was going out for a walk **but** since it was cloudy and chance of mild drizzle so I stayed in.

Consider what a difference the use of **'AND'** would make.

1. I would like to put forward more ideas in the company **and** as my boss is busy I must choose the right time and his right mood.

2. I would like to offer better quality products to my customers **and** therefore I must plan a convincing campaign to show them that they will get better value for their money.

3. I would like to suggest some changes in our society to improve the quality of life **and** as such I must back up my proposal with convincing reasons.

4. I was going out for a walk **and** since it was cloudy with mild drizzle, I took an umbrella and it was great fun as the drizzle stopped midway.

After this exercise the participants are more receptive to the next exercise which is titled as 'What is the real problem?' The participants read out the following statements one by one and after each statement there is a short discussion.

- The problem is **not** the inefficiency and low productivity of my subordinates **but** my inability to train and motivate them.
- The problem is **not** that my subordinates are late **but** my inability to ensure punctuality.
- The problem is **not** that the boss often wastes my time **but** that I have never pointed it out to him in a polite manner.
- The problem is **not** that all the customers are unreasonable **but** my lack of skill in convincing them.
- The problem is **not** the rising price of petrol **but** that I get irritated about things on which I have no control.

And finally I ask them to think over the following two statements:

Negative: The problem is that my wife/husband/ Children never listen to me.

Positive: The real problem is not that they never listen to me, but I do not look for an appropriate time and place and ignore their interest.

I have seen that after these exercises there is some introspection among most participants which is visible from their body language. They start thinking that may be their own mindset and attitude needs some change.

The impact of positive attitude and behaviour was again proved by a study conducted by US NEWS and WORLD to find out why customers are lost. **The findings are an eye opener. The study found that customers are lost because:**

- 1% die
- 3% move to other places
- 5% adopt new habits
- 9% find pricing too high
- 14% are dissatisfied with the product quality but
- **68% are dissatisfied with the attitude and behaviour of the sales staff**

Imagine everything is good about the product or the service and yet we may lose two thirds of the customers because of the attitude of the people who come in contact with the customers.

A good example of what a change from negative to positive attitude can do was experienced by me when I was the Head of Personnel at Rourkela Steel Plant of SAIL.

The Plant Superintendent of Plate Mill always had some reason or other for low productivity and performance without any apparent problem. The matter was discussed at the highest level and it was felt that it was more of an attitude problem. A change was made, the Superintendent was side tracked and one bright General Foreman Brijlal Kshatriya (he later became Managing Director of Bokaro Steel Plant) who was rated as highly positive minded was promoted and appointed as Manager in charge of Plate Mill. Within a span of three months the usual problems – technical as well as human – which used to be quoted in every meeting by the previous plant Head disappeared and the plant started performing better and better.

My next experience of impact of positive attitude also took place during my service with Steel Authority (SAIL). At the beginning of my career I was posted as a junior officer at the Head Office of Hindustan Steel Ltd at Ranchi which was situated in the old Bihar Government Secretariat building. A steno typist Lal and a peon Tiwari were attached to me. Tiwari was very young and may have just completed 18 years. He would sit on a stool outside my office and read a book in his spare time. One day on my asking he told me that he was preparing to appear in the High School examination from Bihar Board privately. After some time he got transferred to some other officer. Later I also got transferred to Durgapur and then to Rourkela Steel Plants. But I kept hearing about him that he had completed his graduation. And one day I heard that he had successfully cleared the written examination of HSL/SAIL for promotion from Non-Executive to

Executive rank and had become a Junior Officer and posted at the Head Office of SAIL in Delhi.

Almost 30 years after my first posting at Ranchi, I was invited by SAIL to conduct a training module of two days in their 'Enhancing Managerial Effectiveness' programme at their Management Training Institute at Ranchi. During my morning walk at the HSL Colony called Shyamali I happened to meet my old Stenotypist Lal and asked him what he was doing. I quote his reply which still rings in my year. "Sir ham to jahan the vanhi hain hamare liye koi kuch nahi karta. Ab Stenographer ho gaye hain" Sir I am in the same position where I was in your time. Nobody does anything for me. Nowadays I am a Stenographer. A few months later I had occasion to visit SAIL headquarters at Lodi Road, New Delhi. Couple of old timers met me and I came to know that Tiwari had become a Manager. So I went his cabin. As soon as he saw me – it must have been after 30 years – he recognised me and got up from his chair with folded hands. I sat down on a chair in front of him but he declined to sit and kept standing. I didn't want to embarrass him. I congratulated him, wished him good luck and left his cabin. But I kept wondering what a difference in attitude can do – positive attitude develops a peon into a manager and negative attitude barely advances a steno typist by one step to a stenographer. This is a real life story with names of persons unchanged.

The lesson is: If we want to achieve success in life let us develop a positive attitude of mind.

CHAPTER 23

Is it worth winning an argument

"Immature people always want to win an argument even at the cost of a relationship. Mature people understand that it's always better to lose an argument and win a relationship."
Anonymous

I was based at Kanpur for three years. The traffic there was a nightmare. You could see all modes of transport on the roads. Moreover no one followed the traffic rules. Even if the road had a divider you could drive on either side of the divider from both sides. This made it chaotic at most of the times. Once when I was returning from the factory at Panki, I saw a big crowd and two cars face to face on the other side of the road. I also noticed that one of the cars belonged to our Manager Naresh (name changed). I got down to see what was happening and also to help Naresh. I found that there were two cars face to face on the same side of the road, with barely a distance of six inches between the cars. From the position of his car I could see that Naresh was driving on the correct side i.e. on the left side of the road divider but the other car was obviously on the wrong side. I asked Naresh what the problem was. Naresh said that the other person was coming from the wrong side and he wanted to correct him. When I talked to the other person he said "In Kanpur it is quite common to drive on any side of the divider and since the other side was busy I was driving on this side but your friend deliberately drove his car in front of my car although there was enough space on the road and he could have easily driven away". I understood what had happened. Naresh was trying his best to prove the other person wrong, but the other person was equally adamant in not moving his car. I took Naresh aside and told him that although he was right and other person was wrong, it was not worth to keep on arguing to prove the other person wrong. And in any case it was the job of a traffic policeman and not his. With great persuasion Naresh agreed to reverse his car and give way to the other car.

My next experience of trying to win an argument took place when my boss and I were travelling together in a car. In the front was our street smart Public Relations Officer. It was a long journey from Ranchi to Dhanbad. Our random and casual talk drifted from one subject to another till we came to Indian History. We started discussing the Mughal Empire and the Mughal dynasty. My boss commented that Akbar was a great King but his son Shahjehan was no match to him. I immediately contradicted and said Shahjehan was not his son. His son was Jahangir. My boss got very upset on this contradiction and told me "OP you should refresh your knowledge of Mughal dynasty". I was about to tell him that it was he who needed refreshing and not me. But in the meantime the driver stopped the car at a petrol pump for filling the petrol tank and my boss went to the washroom. The moment the boss was beyond hearing distance, the smart PRO told me "Sir why are you arguing with the boss unnecessarily. I know that you are right but why are you contradicting the boss? How does it matter whether it was Shahjehan or Jehangir? You need the support of the boss and not of Shahejahan or Jehangir. And in any case the Mughal dynasty is not going to change by your agreeing or disagreeing". I saw his point. In the meantime the boss came back. By now the wise words of smart PRO were ringing in my ears. I told the boss that may be he was right and I was wrong and that I would brush up my knowledge. The boss was happy and we moved on to other subjects. After a couple of days the boss rang me up and said "OP that day you were right about the Mughal dynasty." You can imagine what would have happened if I had insisted on my views that day. The boss would never have agreed and it would have resulted in our strained relationship.

In my next experience, I decided to make use of this lesson. A couple of years ago I received a notice from the Income Tax department that my case has been taken up for scrutiny. I asked my accountant to deal with it. I was upset because I thought that I had done everything above board. When I checked with my accountant I did not get a satisfactory reply. Anyway the case was like this. During the year in question, I had conducted a large number of management training programmes at the Maurya Sheraton Hotel in Delhi. The hotel charges were based on the package which included venue with proper layout of tables and chairs, white board with markers, working lunch, tea/coffee and cold drinks. However the bill mentioned charges for conference lunch. The income tax officer due to some reasons not known to me, decided to treat the entire expense on these bills as entertainment expenses. Consequently he disallowed these as business expense. I went in for appeal. The case was heard by the Appellate Officer of a higher rank. I decided not to argue with the Appellate Officer. Instead I told him "Sir with your vast experience and expertise I leave it to your judgement and I am sure you will do justice". He asked me some factual questions such as the duration of the training programmes, what facilities were included in the charges, were there separate charges for the venue. Once he was satisfied he reversed the order of the ITO and allowed all the expense as business expense.

All the above real life incidents quoted above show that it is not worth trying to win an argument. In fact if you lose the argument you have lost and even if you win you have lost. Because you have hurt the ego and sentiments of the other person and he is not going to digest it easily.

The lesson is: If you want to develop and maintain good relationship with people it is not worth winning an argument.

CHAPTER 24

Accept your mistakes readily

"Mistakes are always forgivable, if one has
the courage to admit them."
Bruce Lee

I regularly play bridge in the City Club of DLF Phase
IV in Gurgaon near Delhi. There is a group of over a
dozen players. During the play, we all make mistakes and
most of us realise our mistake either ourselves or after
somebody points them out. And in most case we accept
our mistakes readily or after some discussion. But I have
seen that one of the players never accepts his mistake.
Whenever anybody points out his mistake he gets upset
and justifies his action in some way or the other. After this
has happened repeatedly others have stopped pointing
out his mistakes but behind his back everybody talks
about him. He remains oblivious to these discussions and
comments. I am sure no one would like to be in such a
position. But this is what happens when we don't accept

our mistakes. We are under the false notion that if we don't accept our mistake others will accept our version.

I once read an article in the Readers' Digest which described an instance in which the mistake was not only accepted but rectified at unimaginable speed. Once a passenger was travelling by Singapore Airlines on a long flight to Singapore. The flight was normal. Lunch time came. The young air hostess started serving drinks. Suddenly there was jerk in the plane and the air hostess stumbled on something and she along with drink fell on the passenger. It spoiled his expensive suit. The air hostess was absolutely nonplussed and highly embarrassed. She kept on repeating "Sir I am extremely sorry" and it went on for some time. The passenger didn't know what to say but his face said whatever he wanted to. This incident must have been noticed or reported to the Head of the cabin crew. She an elderly lady came bowed to the passenger and profusely apologised. She took some time in doing so and carefully watched the passenger and his suit. The passenger didn't know why she was doing it.

The plane landed at Singapore. When the passenger came out from immigration he found a senior member of Singapore Airlines was waiting for him with a packet. He handed over the packet to the passenger and again expressed his regret for the incident during the flight and said that the packet was a gift to him from Singapore Airlines. On reaching home when the passenger opened the packet he found that it contained a brand new suit very similar to the one he was wearing during the flight.

When he put on the suit he was surprised to see that the measurements were perfect and the suit was very comfortable. It is then that he realised why the head of cabin crew was observing him carefully longer than merely to express her apologies. I have narrated the incident as best as I remember which I read more than a decade ago. I may have missed some finer points but the basic story is intact. Why do you think the Singapore Airlines took all this trouble? Your guess is as good as mine. I think they must have realised that for their lapse it is not enough to merely express an apology to the passenger. They must do something better. At the same time they must have decided to make it a model case of not only 'customer satisfaction' or customer delight' but of 'customer surprise'.

Why do you think the auto companies have started a practice of calling back their cars even for minor defects? Toyota has been doing it for quite some time so also other auto companies. In India, Maruti is also following the same practice. The moment these companies come to know of any defect in their product they do not waste any time in recalling it. It increases their trust in the mind of consumers even though at a cost. Surely as long term measure of customer satisfaction, the cost is worth it.

The father of the Nation, Mahatma Gandhi, started his non-cooperation movement against the British. Yet, just as the movement reached its apex, a violent clash took place in February 1922 in the town of Chauri Chaura, Uttar Pradesh. Although non-cooperation movement enjoyed widespread appeal and success, increasing excitement and participation from all strata of Indian society, fearing that the movement was about to take a turn towards violence, and convinced that this would be the undoing of all his work, Gandhiji called off the campaign of mass civil disobedience This was the third time that Gandhiji had called off a major campaign. If a person of the stature of Mahatma Gandhi did not hesitate to accept his mistake of continuing the movement and called it off not once but three times, why are we so reluctant to accept our mistakes? Did Gandhiji lose his face? Or did it improve his stature? You be the judge.

Let us take another example. We are all aware of the Jallianwala massacre at Amritsar on 13 April 1919 in which over 1000 people were killed due to the firing by the British Army on the orders of Brigadier General Dyer. Although Queen Elizabeth II had not made any comments on the incident during her state visits in 1961 and 1983, she spoke about the events at a state banquet in India on 13 October 1997.

"It is no secret that there have been some difficult episodes in our past – Jallianwala Bagh, which I shall visit tomorrow, is a distressing example. But history cannot be rewritten, however much we might sometimes wish otherwise. It has its moments of sadness, as well as gladness. We must learn from the sadness and build on the gladness."

On 14 October 1997, Queen Elizabeth II visited Jallianwala Bagh and paid her respects with a 30second moment of silence. During the visit, she wore a dress of a colour described as pink apricot or saffron, which was of religious significance to the Sikhs. She removed her shoes while visiting the monument and laid a wreath at the monument.

If Queen Elizabeth can express her distress and sadness for an event that took place when she was not even born why can't we do the same for something done by us during our own lifetime?

The lesson we get from all the above examples is this: If you have made a mistake accept it readily and gracefully.

CHAPTER 25

Public speaking - a ladder to success

"A good speech should be like a woman's skirt;
Long enough to cover the subject and short
enough to create interest."
Winston Churchill

I always admired my boss Russi Billimoria for his two qualities, public speaking and public relations. Whenever he would speak in a public forum he would deliver an excellent speech and make an equally good impression. Alas he is no more!! He was my friend philosopher and guide for more than four decades. Once I asked him the secret of his success. In reply he said many things but the one I always remember is his emphasis on "Skill practice". Public speaking is a skill. And all skills require practice. Knowledge can be acquired by reading books or attending lectures but not skill. Suppose you study a manual on swimming thoroughly for four years and then jump into the swimming pool. You know what would happen! Similarly you study a manual on car driving for four years and sit on the driving seat and start the car. Again, you know what would happen! The same is true of public speaking. The more you practice the better you could speak.

In the Parliament elections of 2014 in India the major contributing factor for Narendra Modi's success has been his excellent skill in public speaking. His speeches included all the elements that professionals train in the public speaking training programmes and more. He spoke in the language that the audience could understand, speaking on the issues which interest the audience and which concerns them, pacing and carrying the audience with him by asking them 'Yes' or 'No' and putting the questions in such a way that the answer will always be 'Yes'. And many more. I am sure all this has not happened in one day. It has happened after many years of study and practice. And it has its rewards. A ladder to the high office of the Prime Minister of India.

Apart from listening to Narendra Modi on TV and on YouTube I have had the good fortune of listening to some other top class speeches. Once when I was working at the Durgapur Steel Plant in West Bengal, Jyoti Basu, the then Deputy Chief Minister of west Bengal visited the plant. The industrial relations were tense. Work stoppages and Gheraos were frequent. He was to speak to a gathering of officers in the auditorium. Much before he arrived, the auditorium was full. He came at the announced time but with him came a large contingent of workers who were office bearers and members of his CITU Union. They stood on the sides and also sat down in the front. Jyoti Basu started his speech in English. No sooner had he started there was loud objection from workers who shouted 'Bangla' 'Bangla'. Jyoti Basu stopped and told them in Bengali that he would speak in Bangla also.

The speech that Jyoti Basu gave that day was a masterpiece of oratory. I quote two of his sentences and the reaction from the audience. He said "I am opposed to the violence and 'Gheraos' and these should not take place". There was loud clapping by the officers. His next sentence almost in the same breath was "But all problems and grievance of the workers should be redressed and settled speedily". This time there was loud clapping by the workers. His next sentence would be "Durgapur Steel Plant is the pride of West Bengal; I want it to do well". Clapping from officers. "But it should not mean exploitation of workers". Clapping from workers. I heard this happening alternately a number of times. The speech was also a mix of English and 'Bangla'. Hats off to you Mr. Jyoti Basu. No wonder you remained the Chief Minister of a State for the record number of years – a record which has not been broken so far. One wonders whether it can ever be broken.

My other experience of witnessing the art of public speaking came early in life. I was deputed by the Government of India for training in USA with U.S. Steel Corporation along with attending lectures at the Illinois Institute of

Technology at Chicago. I was living in the International House at Chicago built by Rockefeller for foreign students. Once Dr. S Radhakrishnan visited Chicago when he was the Vice President of India. The India Association organised his lecture at the International House. The hall was full with Indian, American and other foreign students. I was sitting with our American Coordinator Tom Berry and some other friends. Dr. Radhkrishnan started his speech without any written text. He spoke extempore for about an hour on Indian philosophy as well as on India US relations. When the speech ended Tom and some other Americans were wonderstruck. They said they had never heard an American, much less an Indian, speak so well. Due to that speech of Dr. Radhakrishnan the stock of India went up many notches.

The next speech that I remember was delivered by my close friend and colleague in Rourkela Steel Plant Mr. P C Hota IAS (retd.) who eventually became Chairman of the Union Public Service Commission. The speech was delivered in one of my management training programmes on Leadership and Team building at Manali. The programme was to start in the evening and Hota's speech was the inaugural event. Being an outstation programme at a hill station, most of the participants had brought their families. And to keep them engaged, I invited the families also to join the inaugural session. Hota had a difficult job of speaking on leadership and teambuilding and also make it equally interesting for ladies and a few youngsters of families of the participants. I must say he did an excellent job and I rate that speech as good as any other that I have heard.

The last episode of excellent public speaking that I would like to quote happened at Jamshedpur. The occasion was the Convocation of XLRI Jamshedpur. At that time I was the Head of Personnel Department at Rourkela steel Plant. I was invited by Tata Steel to attend the Silver Jubilee celebrations of the Personnel Dept of Tata Steel at Jamshedpur. Both the functions were on the same day. During the convocation function I remember two speeches distinctly. One was by Father Tom, the Director of XLRI. The second was by Mohan Kumarmangalam the Steel Minister. I do not remember the contents of those speeches except the advice of Steel Minister to the passing out management graduates to try to understand the culture of the workforce and their language to be a successful Personnel man. But both the speeches were masterpieces of oratory. We all felt that the time should come to a standstill and that we keep on listening to their oration.

How did all the above master orators acquire their public speaking skill? And what can we do to acquire it? I am summarising the requirement in ten bullet points below.

1. Preparation, preparation and preparation.
2. Analyse the occasion and audience.
3. Gather and select the material to suit Sl. No. 2 above.
4. Use bullet points and avoid verbatim script.

5. Rehearse with friends, family or use a mirror.
6. Start with an attention grabbing statement/remark.
7. Ensure audibility, speak clearly with voice modulation.
8. Maintain eye contact and use gestures.
9. Close with a bang.
10. Practice, practice and practice.

TESTIMONIALS

Due to immense popularity of our soft skills training programme such as Leadership, Team-building, Communication etc. more than 10,000 men and women have attended these programmes with excellent feedback. The 50 most recent testimonials are shown below. These programmes are held mainly in Delhi or Gurgaon. If you are interested in attending any of these programmes please send us an e-mail at hrdcentre@gmail.com and let us know the topics you are interested in. We will inform you about the next available programmes.

1. *"All the sessions were very good….."* **Capt. Dr. Tarun Singhal,** Usha Breco, Ghaziabad (U.P.)
2. *"It is great",* **Kuldeep Verma**, Everest Industries, Roorkee, Uttrakhand.
3. *"It is good as we learned through experience of professionals,* **Umesh Juyal,** Titan Company, Dehradun.
4. *"Good programme"* **H N Vyas**, Ambuja Cements, Rabriyawas, Rajasthan.
5. *"All the speakers are valuable and have experience in the subject"* **Pavan Jain,** Ruchi Soya, Gurgaon.
6. *"All was good, I would like to attend more programmes.."* **Shailza Sharma, Shangri-La's Eros Hotel,** New Delhi
7. *"Programme was good and best for our knowledge …"* **Kavita Dhoundiyal,** Vodafone, New Delhi
8. *"The programme construct was good…."* **Shivangi Rautela,** Vodafone, New Delhi

9. *"Entire programme was valuable"* **Sudhanshu Jha**, Lupin Lab, Mandideep, (M.P)

10. *"All sessions are most valuable for me"* **Rajeev Kumar Shukla,** O.P.Jindal Global University, Sonipat (Haryana).

11. *"Programme was detailed and good."* **Aman Soni,** Asian Paints, Rohtak (Haryana)

12. *"Programme was very useful"* **Rakesh Kumar Sharma,** Bharat Electronics, Panchkula, (Haryana)

13. *"Overall programme* was *excellent"* **Rampal Singh Yadav**, NTN Mfg. India, Bawal, Bhiwadi, (Haryana)

14. *"Very good interactive sessions"* **Rahul Nigam,** Lupin Pharmaceuticals, Mandideep (M.P.)

15. *"The entire programme was informative and practical"* **Sanjay Goyal**, Bajaj Hindusthan, Palia Kalan, Kheri (U.P.)

16. *"Programme is very good and faculty are very knowledgeable"* **Rajul Trivedi**, JK Lakshmi Cement, Gandhinagar (Gujarat)

17. *"It was a good programme"* **Saurabh Singh**, Pepsico India Holdings Pvt. Ltd. Gurgaon (Haryana)

18. *"Very nice session, able to learn so many things in a new way"* **Rekha Joshi,** Mother Dairy, Noida (U.P.)

19. *"It was a wonderful programme"* **Kishor Nahar,** Newgen Software Technologies Ltd. New Delhi

20. *"This is already a well-designed programme. Keep it up."* **Shailesh Shukla,** UFLEX Ltd. Noida (U.P.)

21. *"This programme very useful for all HR professionals"* **Shailendra Bepari**, TAFE Motors & Tractors. Mandideep (M.P.)

22. *"Sessions and coverage were quite adequate"* **Sanjay Kumar**, Tata Steel Ltd. Jamshedpur

23. *"I think this is the best way"* **A. B. Pandey**, Alstom India Ltd. Durgapur (W.B.)

24. *"All the sessions were good, well designed and crisp"* **Vinay Prakash Singh**, Arshia International Ltd. Khurja, (U.P.)

25. *"Programme is very well designed. Keep it up".* **Vivek Singh**, Uniparts India Ltd. Noida, (U.P.)

26. *"Programme is very well managed..Good programme"* **Kalpesh Bhagat** JBF Industries, Valsad, (Gujarat)

27. *"Overall a good programme"* **Davinder Singla**, Bharat Electronics Ltd. Panchkula (Haryana)

28. *"Faculty should be like Mr. O.P.Khetan"* **N.S. Dadwal**,Ambuja Cement Ltd.. Ropar (Punjab)

29. *"The programme was very informative..."* **Rekha Bakshi,** Tata Chemicals, Noida (U.P.)

30. *"Excellent two days sessions..."* **Praveen Sharma**, TEVA API India Ltd. Greater Noida (U.P.)

31. *"Programme is very useful and knowledgeable. Please keep it up."* **I. K. Ganotra**, Aravali Power Co. Pvt. Ltd. Noida (U.P.)

32. *"The entire programme was beautifully designed and topic nicely covered"* **Shruti Parashar**, Neemrana Hotels, New Delhi

33. *"Overall programme was very good"* **Ratan Lal** IFFCO, Allahabad

34. *"Everything found very fantastic"* **Sanjeev Kumar** Caparo Maruti, Gurgaon, (Haryana)

35. *"This is very good programme...."* **M.P.Singh** Tata Marcopolo, Lucknow

36. *"Very professionally managed. Absolutely befitting."* **M R Mishra** NALCO, Damanjodi, (Orissa)

37. *"All the sessions were valuable."* **Col. Sandeep Khanna** ATS Services, New Delhi

38. *"This programme will be beneficiary in future because it is very effective"* **K N Pathak**, Teva API India, Gajraula (U.P.)

39. *"The programme is really effective...."* **C. Vijayan,** Grasim Industries, Vikram Cement, Khor (M.P.)

40. *"As per me, the programme was very effective and easily understandable"* **Dinesh Zale,** Ericsson India Pvt. Ltd., Jaipur

41. *"Overall this programme is very useful in all aspects"* **Santosh Kumar**, International Auto Ltd., Jamshedpur

42. *"The programme is very well managed/systematic..."* **Sameer Bhatia,** Knorr-Bremse India, Faridabad, (Haryana)

43. *"All the sessions were excellent"* **S Sabanaygan,** J.K.Industies, New Delhi

44. *"The programme is very good"* **Pramod Kumar Ghosh,** Hindalco Industries, Hirakud (Orissa)

45. *"This programme is really effective ..."* **Aurobindo Mishra,** Small Industries Dev. Bank of India, Lucknow

46. *"This programme is very useful in all aspects for all industries ..."* **R P Tripathi** Threads India Kanpur

47. *"It was organised well with sufficient exercises and material"* **S.Sugumar,** Godrej Consumer Products, Malanpur (M.P.)

48. *"It is very good programme and the presentation is also very positive"* **S.C.Viz** Ranbaxy, SAS Nagar, (Punjab)

49. "I feel that the programme was very well structured" **Shivani Kapoor,** Hindustan Lever, Gurgaon, (Haryana)

50. *"Overall good and more than Expectations"* **Ashok Khurana,** JCB India, Ballabhgarh, (Haryana)

YOUR EXPERIENCE MAY HELP OTHERS

I am sure you must have had many similar experiences as quoted in this book. If you would like to help others by sharing such experiences, please write to us. We will try to include all such experiences in our next edition. Please also let us know if your name and the places mentioned in your real life experience are to be kept confidential or disclosed in the book. We will follow your instructions. Who knows your experience may help others to lead a happier and more successful life.

O. P. Khetan
Executive Director, HRD Centre
512-B Hamilton Court,
DLF City Phase IV
Gurgaon 122009
India

E-mail: hrdcentre@gmail.com